HISTORY BYTES

People, Places, and Events That Shaped American History

TABLE OF CONTENTS

GETTING STARTED

One of the sad facts of history is that not everything you know about the past is altogether true. In fact, many of the things you learn about American history in elementary school and high school are an outright lie.

"How can that be, you ask?" I read it in my textbook, and the teacher said it was true. "Why would they lie to me?"

Good question, and one I'm going to attempt to answer throughout this book.

The truth is much of what we learn about history is a series of little white lies that over time have grown into tall tales.

George Washington didn't walk around with a mouthful of wooden teeth. Those are real teeth and pearl inlays in Washington's dentures. A recent study by Mary Thompson suggests Washington experimented with early dental transplants. He purchased replacement teeth from his slaves for thirteen shillings (roughly $50 in 2015 money).

Another truth every school child learns early on is Paul Revere was a great hero of the Revolution and saved the day by alerting the Minutemen at Lexington and Concord that the British were coming.

It's true. Paul Revere made a midnight ride, and he spread the news about the British advance on Lexington and Concord, but the fact is—

Revere never completed his mission that night. And, here's another fact no one bothers to mention. Revere wasn't the only one to make that ride. A second rider, William Dawes, set out by land at the same time Revere rowed across the bay to Charlestown.

And, one of the biggest hoaxes ever played on Americans occurred during the 1930s and early 1940s. FDR had polio and could barely walk, yet during his presidency, most Americans had no idea the president was disabled.

American history is full of strange paradoxes. That's one of the things that make it so enjoyable.

Why doesn't everyone know that Mrs. Woodrow Wilson virtually ran the country during the final days of his administration? Wilson had a massive stroke and was bedridden for the last year and a half of his presidency.

The six o'clock news makes a big deal about cars crashing through White House gates, and crazed lunatics jumping over White House fences, but none of those newscasts have flashed back to the shootout at Blair House on November 1st, 1950.

Two men approached Blair House from opposite directions and opened fire on White House Police and Secret Service agents stationed there. Over thirty rounds were fired in less than three minutes.

Three White House guards were wounded. Another one died later that day from injuries he received in the gun battle. One of the gunmen, Griselio Torresola, took a bullet in the head and died. Another, Oscar Collazo, was shot down on the steps of Blair House but survived.

President Truman watched the entire incident play out from an upstairs bedroom, as two gunmen stormed the temporary executive mansion with their guns blazing. An hour after the shooting ended,

Truman delivered a speech at Arlington National Cemetery, apparently un-phased by the incident.

Talk about cojones.

STORIES OF THE DISCOVERERS

One fact we are sure of as kids is "Christopher Columbus sailed the ocean blue in fourteen hundred and ninety-two." He expected to discover a new route to the Indies. Instead, he sailed head on into a previously unknown continent landing at San Salvador Island in the Bahamas.

That's what we've been taught for hundreds of years. Hell! We even created a special day just to celebrate his discoveries.

Recent scholarship, however, tells a different story about who the actual discoverer of America was.

....

If the truth is told, Columbus was late to the party.

The actual discoverers may have been the ancient Phoenicians, who are supposed to have sailed to America as early as two thousand years ago. Mark McMenamin contends the images on a Phoenician gold coin dating from 350 BC shows a horse with a tiny map of the world under it. And, you guessed it—America is pictured on that map. Another piece of evidence is credited to a Sicilian historian, Diodorus, writing in the first century BC, "...in the deep off Africa is an island of considerable size…The Phoenicians had discovered it by accident after having planted many colonies throughout Africa."

St. Brendan was an Irish monk, who legend has it, voyaged to America as early as the sixth century. Of course, Brendan wasn't looking for America, either. He assumed he could sail his way to paradise, and discover heaven on earth. What Brendan found instead, was an island so big after forty days of walking he was unable to cross it. He found a "river too wide to be crossed," a "floating island," and "an island of fire" that pelted him with rocks.

The best claim to being the original discoverer of North America belongs to a Viking sailor named Leif Eriksson. Archaeological evidence suggests the Vikings had a settlement at L' Anse Aux Meadows in Newfoundland dating back to 1,000 AD.

Before I go further into the story of the discovery, I feel a compelling need to point out—America was never lost, so in reality, it never needed to be found. North America was populated by millions of Native Americans when the first discoverers arrived. In their quest for riches, it never occurred to them the original inhabitants may have had a claim to the lands they inhabited.

But that's a story for another book.

WAS AN IRISH SAINT THE FIRST EUROPEAN TO SET FOOT ON AMERICAN SOIL?

One of the most fantastical accounts in the annals of discovery is the *Navigatio Sancti Brendani* or the *Voyages of Saint Brendan*. It was first written down in the ninth century and tells the story of St. Brendan's seven-year search for paradise on Earth.

Many scholars dismiss the *Navigatio* because it reads more like science fiction than fact, but others believe there are hints of truth buried deep within the story.

This much we know.

St. Brendan was born near Tralee, in County Kerry, in Ireland in 484 AD. He was ordained at age 28 and preached the Gospels in Scotland, Wales, and Brittany. During his travels, he established monasteries at Ardfert, Shanakeel, Kilbrandon, and Kilbrennan Sound.

At the monastery on Donegal Bay, Brendan met an abbot, Father Barinthus, who said he had made many visits to the "Isle of the Saints," and that it was just a short voyage away. After many talks with the abbot, Brendan set sail for the "Island of Paradise."

To make the journey, he constructed a 30-foot currach, a traditional round bottomed Irish boat. The vessel had square sails. Its wooden frame was covered with water-tight seal skins to protect it.

There are over 100 versions of the story, so it's difficult to sort fact from fiction. Most accounts say, Brendan, sailed from Dingle Bay in Ireland with 16 monks, though some say it was closer to 160 voyagers.

Before setting off, the monks fasted for forty days in three-day intervals. When they started their journey, they had no idea where the "Island of Paradise" was. They trusted in God that he would lead them to it.

Along the way, they met with all sorts of adventures, many of which make the stories of Sinbad's journeys seem like child's play.

After 40 days, there appeared before them an island that was very rocky and steep. The "cliffs stood upright like a wall." They sailed around the island for three days until God guided them to a landing place. Once on land, they discovered a dog who led them to a large mansion. That night after supper Brendan was visited by a demon in the shape of a "black boy." In the morning, the monks left the island.

On another island, they found flocks of sheep that were "pure white" and so numerous they "hid the face of the land." They met a servant of God who gave them a basket of hearth-cakes and directed them to an island called the "Paradise of Birds" where more food would be waiting for them. In their flight, the birds made "a tinkling sound like little bells." The birds told Brendan they were fallen creatures doomed to live on the island, and that Brendan had now been on his journey for one year. They prophesized it would take him six more years to complete his quest.

Next, they were "tossed about to and fro on the billows of the ocean" for three months. A fish of enormous size swam after the boat, "spouting foam from its nostrils, and ploughing through the waves in rapid pursuit to devour them." Brendan ordered the frightened monks to fear not. God would protect them. They landed on a nearby island and took three months' provisions of food from the beast.

On another occasion, they watched a giant Gryphon swoop down upon them. Out of nowhere, a second Gryphon appeared. The giant Gryphons battled in midair and crashed dead into the ocean.

Immediately after the ordeal with the Gryphons, they encountered an island Brendan described as being on the "confines of hell." They heard the noise of "bellows blowing like thunder, and the beating of sledges on anvils of iron." Soon after that, a hairy and hideous looking beast raced towards them, showering the monks with a mass of burning slag. As they rowed away from the island, more of the horrid creatures gathered along the shore. They continued to pelt the brethren with fire and brimstone as they sailed away.

After seven days at sea, Brendan discovered another island. This one, inhabited by Judas Iscariot, the disciple who betrayed Jesus to the Romans. Judas recounted the story of being in his private hell and the sufferings he had endured.

On the next stop, they discovered a small round island inhabited by a hermit who lived in a cave. The man, "was covered all over from head to foot with the hair of his body, which was white as snow from old age, and no other garment had he save this." The hermit surprised the brethren, greeting each of them by their given name.

Not long after this, they reached the "Promised Land of the Saints."

It was an amazing land where night time was banished, and daylight ruled. A thick layer of vegetation and fruits covered the ground. The brethren traveled for forty days with no end of land in sight, until they eventually came to a "river too large to cross."

While they pondered what to do next, a handsome young man appeared before them. He told Brendan, "This is the land you have sought after for so long a time…After many years this land will be made manifest to those who come after you." With that, the young man invited Brendan to gather all the fruit and precious stones his boat could carry. He told Brendan to return to the land of his birth, for "the days of your earthly pilgrimage must draw to a close, when you may rest in peace among your saintly brethren."

Brendan returned to his monastery at Ardfert after seven years of travels. Historians speculate he may have visited Iceland, Greenland, and possibly the American coast. Stories of St. Brendan's travels circulated widely throughout medieval Europe. Many scholars think Columbus decided to sail west, based in part on information contained in the *Navigatio Sancti Brendani.*

. . . .

Set aside all the religious references, and exaggerated claims. Was such a trip possible? Could St. Brendan, and his crew, have sailed across the Atlantic in a 30-foot Irish currach.

To test this idea, explorer Timothy Severin constructed a vessel like the one described in the *Navigatio.* He charted a course similar to Brendan's and was able to sail across the Atlantic. That was in 1976. But, the real question is, just because Timothy Severin was able to recreate the voyage, does that mean Brendan could have done it, too?

That's a question we will probably never answer. Unlike the Vikings, the Irish never colonized North America, so it is unlikely any archeological evidence will surface to solidify the Irish claim to discovery.

My regrets to the Irish, but the Brendan voyages are most likely nothing more than blarney.

NORSE DISCOVERIES IN GREENLAND, ICELAND, AND NEWFOUNDLAND

Author's note: Most of what I know about Vikings I learned as a child, from reading Hägar the Horrible. Some of you might remember the comic strip drawn by Dik Browne, and later, after his death by his son, Chris Browne. Hägar wasn't your typical Viking. He wore a brown burlap bag style outfit (more suited to a cave dweller than a Viking), sported a bushy red beard, and he always wore that horned cap we associate with the Vikings. Hägar spent most of his time raiding England and France, but when he could spare a few moments, he hung with his friend Lucky Eddie, and his dog Snert.

....

Legend has it the Vikings established colonies in North America, but there was no hard evidence to support these claims until 1960. That year archaeologists uncovered a Norse settlement on the northern tip of Newfoundland at L'Anse Aux Meadows.

Archaeologist say L'Anse Aux Meadows wasn't the Vinland settlement founded by Leif Eriksson around 1,000 AD. It is more likely

L'Anse was a stopping off point for travelers and traders on their way from Greenland to the North American continent.

L'Anse Aux Meadows consisted of three Norse longhouses, several workshops, an iron forge, and an iron smelter. It would have housed around 75 inhabitants. Archeologists think it was a temporary settlement, used for just a few years. As evidence to support this, scientists point out they didn't discover any garbage dumps, burial sites, or bodies nearby.

. . . .

What we do know about the Norse settlers in Greenland and Newfoundland is they weren't the typical blood and guts type Vikings you usually think of. Unlike *Hägar the Horrible,* they weren't fierce warriors on a quest to conquer new lands. They were livestock farmers, who raised sheep and goats because the land was not suited for growing grains.

Archeological evidence suggests they didn't sail the classic Norse longboats used by Viking raiders. Instead, they voyaged there in the Knarr. The Knarr was a more seaworthy vessel the Vikings sailed on longer journeys. It had a wider hull and was smaller than the Viking longboat. As a result, it could carry more cargo and required a smaller crew.

In 982 Erik the Red was banned from Iceland for three years because of some murders he committed. While looking for a new place to live he discovered Greenland, so named for the trees and grass he found along the coast. When his banishment ended in 985, Erik the Red returned to Iceland and recruited a large group of colonists to settle Greenland with him. Twenty-five boats, loaded with five hundred men, women, children, and supplies ventured there to establish a new life on Greenland. They established two settlements—one at Brattahild headed by Erik the Red, and the other at Nuuk. They were known as the East and West Settlements.

The *Greenland Sagas* say Bjarni Herjolfsson made the first sighting of the North American coast in 986. He was blown off course and spotted a heavily forested coastline that appeared unfamiliar to him. Herjolfsson didn't take time out to explore the new lands he discovered. He was anxious to get back to Greenland and return to business as usual. He did, however, tell other voyagers about the areas he'd found.

Around 1000, Erik the Red's son, Leif Eriksson returned to Greenland. He brought the first Christian missionaries to Greenland. Soon after his return his mother converted to Christianity and established the first Christian church in Greenland at Brattahild.

After this, the story gets a little fuzzy.

Some accounts, say Leif Eriksson was blown off course, and accidentally landed on the North American coast. Other reports suggest, Eriksson heard the stories about Bjarni Herjolfsson's discoveries and set off to Christianize the natives of those lands as commanded by King Olaf I. Since the *Greenland Sagas* say Eriksson made the voyage in Bjarni Herjolfsson's boat, it is likely he intended to retrace Herjolfsson's voyage.

Leif Eriksson made three landfalls in the new world.

The first, on a rocky and desolate coast (most likely Baffin Island). He named the area Helluland. His second stop was in a forested area he called Markland (thought to be Southern Labrador). Eriksson's final stop was called Vinland because of the grape vines he discovered there. Over a thousand years later the exact location of Vinland is still a mystery. Historians have pegged it anywhere from New York to Newfoundland.

At the end of his voyages, Leif Eriksson sailed back to Greenland with a cargo of grapes and timber. He never returned to Vinland.

Seven years after Leif Eriksson's voyage, Thorfinn Karlsefni and his wife Gudrid voyaged to Newfoundland. Their son, Snorri, was the first

European child born in North America. The settlement consisted of roughly 100 people. Most likely they built traditional Norse style longhouses with sod walls and peaked roofs made of timber and stone.

The colony came under constant attack from the local natives, whom they called *Skraelings*, or "the wretched people." The *Skraelings* were a fierce, warlike people and didn't get along with the Norsemen. They mounted constant attacks on the villagers that prevented them from making progress with their settlement.

After three years, the Vikings abandoned their North American colonies and returned to their homes in Greenland and Iceland.

CHRISTOPHER COLUMBUS - ORIGINAL DISCOVER OF AMERICA, OR LATE TO THE PARTY?

Christopher Columbus (born Christopher Colon) is a complex character. On the one hand, Columbus was deeply religious and believed God had inspired his voyages of discovery. On the other hand, he was incredibly cruel and allowed the wanton massacre of the native races for the amusement of his men.

After meeting the Arawak natives, Columbus wrote in his journal, "With fifty men we could subjugate them all and make them do whatever we want."

Later, as governor of Hispaniola, Columbus set a quota for native workers. If they did not bring him a set amount of gold dust, his men lopped off their hands and tied them around their necks after which they were left to wander and suffer until they bled to death. Records show 10,000 unfortunate men, women, and children suffered this fate.

And that is only the start of the atrocities.

Bartolomé de las Casas traveled with Columbus on several of his voyages and later wrote about the horrors he witnessed on Hispaniola. "They [Columbus's men] laid Wagers among themselves, who should with a Sword at one blow cut, or divide a Man in two; or which of them should decollate or behead a Man…They snatcht young Babes from the

Mothers Breasts, and then dasht out the brains of those innocents against the Rock."

Most of what we learn about Christopher Columbus is incorrect.

Neither Columbus nor most of the scientific world believed the Earth was flat. The ancient Greeks proved the Earth was spherical as early as the sixth century BC. So, all that crap about the risk Columbus took, and how his ships might fall off the edge of the Earth to certain death. Don't believe it.

It is true, Columbus had trouble finding backers to finance his first voyage of discovery. Portugal, England, and France all turned him down before Spain funded his first voyage. It's also true, Columbus kept two sets of records—one that was accurate, and one that he shared with his men. In the logbook he shared with his crew, Columbus shortened the distance he traveled, to quell dissatisfaction and mutiny. The real problem was—Columbus misestimated the size of the Earth by about twenty-five percent. Much of the reason for this was he didn't realize the continents of North and South America existed.

Here's another fact not commonly discussed. Columbus's first voyage to America took 43 days. Living conditions for his sailors were pure hell. Most of his men walked around barefoot during the entire trip. They wore the same clothes home that they started out with. Rats shared the decks, sleeping quarters, and food with the crew, and no one escaped the many lice infestations.

On Christmas Eve 1492, a cabin boy steered the Santa Maria into a coral reef and wrecked it. That incident forced Columbus to leave thirty-nine men behind when he returned to Spain. The sailors left behind formed the settlement of *La Navidad*, the first European colony in the Americas.

Over the next ten years, Columbus made three more voyages to America. Contrary to common belief, Columbus never set foot in the continental United States, nor did he understand he had discovered a new continent. Throughout his life, Columbus insisted his ships landed in the Orient. The mistaken belief he had landed in India caused Columbus to name the native inhabitants *Indios*, later Americanized to *Indians*.

In 1500, Christopher Columbus, who was then serving as governor of Hispaniola, was arrested and brought back to Spain in chains. The charges included cruelty to the native inhabitants, the execution of rebel Spanish colonists, and mismanagement of the colony. After a short trial, he was found not guilty. The only real consequence was he was removed as governor of Hispaniola. Whatever, the Spanish crown thought of the charges leveled against Columbus, it couldn't have taken them too seriously because King Ferdinand financed Columbus's fourth voyage in 1502.

Late in his life, Columbus wrote a controversial book titled *The Book of Prophecies*. In it, he said God, directed his explorations. He proclaimed the end of the world would soon be at hand. Mysteriously, he took credit for it, saying "he was causing it."

Whatever can be said about Christopher Columbus, his voyages ushered in a new age of discovery and economic expansion in Europe. He also unleashed an era of unending cruelty, death, and destruction for the native inhabitants of the new world. One can't help but wonder if he had treated the natives more humanely, would there have been a different outcome in the colonization of the new world?

AMERIGO'S LAND – HOW AMERICA GOT ITS NAME

Naming a continent is a funny thing.

One man is the acknowledged discoverer of an entirely new world, yet by pure chance, another receives credit for his discovery.

History tells us German cartographer, Martin Waldseemüller, scribbled *America* over the country of Brazil on a new map he was working on in 1507. He'd read Vespucci's account of his discoveries, and decided it would be a good way to honor the navigator and discoverer of that area.

Waldseemüller said, he wrote the word *America* across Brazil on the new map because, "I see no reason why anyone should justly object to calling this part America, after Amerigo [Vespucci] its discoverer, a man of great ability."

Over time, the name just sort of stuck.

In 1538, the famed mapmaker Gerardus Mercator extended the name to all North and South America. From that point on, Amerigo Vespucci's, *Novus Mundo*, or new world, would bear his name.

. . . .

Amerigo Vespucci was born March 9th, 1454, in Florence, Italy. As a young man, he worked as a clerk for Lorenzo de' Medici. In 1492 he traveled to Cadiz, Spain to serve as an agent in that branch. In 1495 Vespucci helped procure supplies for Columbus's second voyage.

Vespucci switched allegiances in 1499 and began work for the King of Portugal. He participated in several voyages of discovery. Some say he acted as an observer for the king; other accounts contend he was a navigator on several of the voyages. Whichever account is true; Vespucci was present on several critical voyages of discovery.

The voyage of 1501-1502 convinced Vespucci it was a "new world" he had discovered—not Asia. And, that is one of the fundamental differences between Christopher Columbus and Amerigo Vespucci. Columbus always believed he had reached the Indies. Amerigo Vespucci took a leap of faith and determined he'd discovered a new continent, one unknown in Ptolemaic geography.

The second difference between Amerigo Vespucci and Christopher Columbus is Vespucci penned a series of letters and books detailing his travels. In his letters, Vespucci proclaimed he had discovered a new world, one he named *Mundus Novus*.

In his pamphlet on the subject, Vespucci wrote, "I have found a continent more densely peopled and abounding in animals than our Europe or Asia or Africa, and, in addition, a climate milder and more delightful than in any other region known to us…We knew that land to be a continent and not an island both because it stretches forth in the form of a very long and unbending coast and because it is replete with infinite inhabitants."

His descriptions of the natives he encountered were quite detailed, down to their marriage customs, sex lives, eating habits, and daily activities. In another of his letters, Vespucci wrote, "…they eat little flesh except human flesh…they are so inhuman that they outdo every custom (even) of beasts; for they eat all their enemies whom they kill or capture."

Many historians insist much of Vespucci's letters and books were fabricated or written by others, but this much is true: Vespucci's books were the talk of Europe. They sold better than the works of Columbus and were much more popular.

The result is *Mundus Novus*, or the new world became Amerigo's land or *America*.

And, that's the story of how America got its name.

. . . .

Of course, there is a conflicting claim.

Alfred Hudd, an amateur historian, presented a theory in 1908. He suggested John Cabot was the first European explorer to reach North America. Hudd said Cabot sailed past Iceland in 1497, in search of new fishing grounds for Bristol merchants shut out of the Icelandic fishing trade since 1475, when the King of Iceland banned foreign fisherman from fishing in his country's waters.

Hudd said, John Cabot sailed to Newfoundland in 1497, on the ship Matthew, provided by his patron Richard Amerike (AKA Ameryk).

On that voyage, Cabot mapped the coastline between Nova Scotia and Newfoundland. By custom, he further assumed Cabot would have named the new found lands after his patron. Thus, Amerike or Ameryk became twisted into America, and he is the actual namesake of America, not Amerigo Vespucci.

Hudd's only evidence was a passing glance at a lost manuscript he'd seen years before—an early calendar of local events. Supposedly, it recorded that on June 24th, 1497, "the land of America was found by merchants of Bristol" in a Bristol ship, the Matthew.

26

The problem is—the evidence burned up in a subsequent fire.

That theory received a new breath of life in 2006 when *The Book of General Ignorance was published*. The authors claim Cabot mapped the shorelines between Nova Scotia and Newfoundland in 1497, ten years before Martin Waldseemüller published his map and four years before Amerigo Vespucci made his first voyage to the new world.

Again, there's no proof the new land was called America, just the theory that John Cabot would have named any discoveries after his patron.

So, there you have it.

America was either named after Amerigo Vespucci because an obscure mapmaker read an account of his voyages, and later mapmakers accepted the name, or after a Bristol merchant who sent an expedition in search of new fishing grounds.

At this late date, we may as well flip a coin to make the final decision. Heads Amerigo Vespucci, tails Richard Amerike.

JAMESTOWN – CAPTAIN JOHN SMITH & POCAHONTAS

The Jamestown saga has all the ingredients of a classic thriller—intrigue, adventure, Indian attacks, starvation, slavery, and cannibalism.

Every school child has heard the story of Captain John Smith, and his timely rescue by the beautiful Indian maiden Pocahontas. Smith was out hunting with two other settlers when Indians ambushed them. The natives killed Smith's companions, and took him, prisoner. Chief Powhatan sentenced him to be clubbed to death in a ritual ceremony, but at the last minute—twelve-year-old Pocahontas, the favorite daughter of Powhatan, threw herself in front of Smith and demanded the chief spare his life.

After this, the story gets a little shaky.

The entire premise of the story rests upon this paragraph from Smith's *The Generall Historie of Virginia* published in 1624. *"Two great stones were brought before Powhatan: then as many as could layd hands on him [Smith], dragged him to them, and thereon laid his head, and being ready with their clubs, to beate out his brains, Pocahontas the King's dearest daughter, when no intreaty could prevaile, got his head in her armes, and laid her own upon his to save him from death; whereat the emperour was contented he should live."*

The fact is, the incident probably never happened, no told it anyway.

Several problems exist with the story. 1) Smith was the only wi. to the incident, and he didn't mention anything about the rescue in any of his earlier accounts, and 2) Current historians contend if the event did occur; it was more of an adoption ritual practiced by the Indians, rather than an attempt to kill Smith.

Again, it's all in how you look at it. If Smith didn't know the Algonquian customs, it would appear to him that Pocahontas stepped in to save his life. So, it seems likely the story we tell ourselves about Captain John Smith and Pocahontas is more of a fairy tale than a real event.

. . . .

Here's another little-known fact. England was cash poor at the opening of the 16th Century, and unable to finance far-flung colonies in the new world. King James I granted a charter to the **Virginia Company** in 1606 allowing them to establish a colony in North America.

Three boats containing 105 colonists sailed from London on December 20th, 1606—the *Susan Constant*, *Godspeed*, and *Discovery*. After a four-month voyage, they reached the shores of the Chesapeake Bay. It took another two weeks of exploration to select the area around Jamestown for the new settlement. The site was chosen because it was inland, and enclosed on three sides, so it was easily defensible in case of attacks by Spanish privateers.

Attacks by the native tribes occurred within the first few days of the colonists' arrival.

The settlers set up a hurried wooden fort. It was a triangular shaped structure with bulwarks (raised platforms) on each side to mount cannons for protection in case of an attack. Inside the walls of the fort, the colonists built a warehouse, church, and several houses.

Times were tough for the new settlers. Food was scarce, yet no one took the time to plant crops. Everyone was intent on striking it rich and set out searching for silver and gold, rather than tending to their basic needs—first. The Virginia Company launched the colony with the expectation of finding hordes of treasure like the Spanish explorers had discovered in South America, Mexico, and the American southwest.

Later that summer Captain Christopher Newport returned to England with two ships and forty men, to restock supplies and recruit more colonists. Newport returned in October of 1608 with 70 new settlers, and the first women to live in the colony.

In 1608 Captain John Smith became president of the Council. He was a firm disciplinarian and issued an edict to address the constant food shortages. "He that will not work shall not eat." He encouraged farming and used his influence with Powhatan, and the Algonquian tribes to secure much-needed food supplies.

A rat infestation overtook the colony in April of 1609. The rats destroyed most of the colonist's food. Smith ordered everyone to work or be thrown out of the fort. He sent other colonists to trade with the natives for fruit and other assorted foodstuffs.

In early summer of 1609, a provision ship arrived with wine and food. In August of 1609 more ships arrived bringing 300 new settlers. Then in October of that same year, Smith received serious injuries in a gunpowder explosion while leading an exploration party. He sailed to England to recover, and never returned to Jamestown.

The winter of 1609/1610 almost saw the annihilation of the colony. The natives—disturbed by the increasing population of the white settlers, and their constant demands for land and food, laid siege to the fort. Things got so bad; the settlers ate horses, boots, rats, and other vermin. One inhabitant, George Percy, later wrote times were so desperate some people dragged the dead out of their graves and devoured the bodies.

It is estimated 80 percent of the population or roughly 240 people died that winter, since designated, as *"the starving times."*

The new Governor, Baron De La Warr, arrived on June 10, 1610. He brought more settlers and much-needed supplies. Conflict with the Algonquians escalated, and a new series of Indian wars broke out. They only stopped when Samuel Argall captured Pocahontas. Upon her capture, Powhatan sued for peace, and a brief period of calm settled over the colony.

In 1611 Baron De La Warr was replaced as Governor by Sir Thomas Gates. Gates enforced strict trade rules with the natives and began a series of attacks on the Algonquians burning their villages, destroying crops, and wantonly killing many Indians. In 1614, John Rolfe, a prominent tobacco planter, married Pocahontas, and a brief period of peace with the natives ensued.

The first blacks arrived in Jamestown in 1619 as cargo from a captured Portuguese slaver. Fifty of them were sold into indentured servitude to pay for their passage to the colony. Pocahontas visited England and died on the return voyage in 1617. Chief Powhatan died in 1618, and his brother Chief Opchanacanough started a new series of attacks on the colonists. In 1622 Opchanacanough launched a major offensive against the colony that killed 25 percent of its population, or nearly 400 men, women, and children.

King James I, revoked the Virginia Company's charter in 1624 and made Jamestown the first Royal Colony in North America.

REVOLUTIONARY PERIOD

Most of us think the American Revolution** began when the Founding Fathers signed the Declaration of Independence on July 4th, 1776. But, that's not accurate. The movement towards independence had its beginnings as early as the French & Indian Wars. After seven years of fighting, the British Crown was nearly bankrupt and needed to create new revenue streams to refill its treasury.

To that end, they imposed a series of taxes on the American colonies—the Stamp Act, the Sugar Act, the Tea Tax, and the various Currency Acts. Most of these taxes were minor, often just a few pence, so it wasn't so much the taxes that got the colonists dander up, as it was the reasoning behind them. Before the Stamp Act any taxes imposed on the colonies were for one purpose only—to regulate trade. These new taxes were different—the purpose behind them was to raise revenue for the Crown.

And, that worried the Colonists. If the Crown could impose taxes on documents, sugar, and tea, they began to wonder—what would Parliament tax next?

The other thing most people don't understand is the first cry for independence didn't come from upper-class planters or the middle class—

it came from the rabble and the poor. Even though George Washington is considered the Father of Our Country; that title could just as easily go to Samuel Adams. Without Samuel Adams, there may have never been an American Revolution. Instead of its signature burger, McDonald's main dish could be tea and crumpets.

The fact is, Sam Adams was a failure at most everything he ever attempted. He had one ruling passion—politics. And, he had the support of Benjamin Edes, the publisher of the *Boston Gazette*, to help spread his ideas. Together they were a powerful force for change.

Sam Adams and John Hancock founded the first chapter of the Sons of Liberty in 1765. By the end of the year, there was a chapter in each of the thirteen colonies. The Sons of Liberty played a significant role in every event leading up to the Revolution. Their members played an instrumental part in the Stamp Act protest, the Boston Massacre, and the Boston Tea Party.

Finally, I decided to examine two legends of the Revolution, Paul Revere, and Betsy Ross. Until the Centennial Celebration in 1876, Ross and Revere were virtually unknown to most Americans. Poet, Henry Wadsworth Longfellow rescued Paul Revere from obscurity. Betsy Ross was brought to national attention by her grandson, William Canby, during an address he made to the Pennsylvania Historical Society in 1870.

STAMP ACT CONGRESS, SONS OF LIBERTY, AND THE BIRTH OF A NATIONAL SPIRIT

Have you ever noticed how sometimes the littlest acts create the biggest consequences?

England found itself strapped for cash at the close of the *Seven Years War* (known in the colonies as the *French and Indian Wars)* and saw the Stamp Act as a method to generate some much-needed revenue.

When members of Parliament passed the Stamp Act on March 22, 1765, they didn't give it a second thought. The tax was quite minor. It was expected to raise roughly £60,000 pounds, less than one-fifth of what it cost the Crown to keep troops stationed in North America for the protection of the colonies. And, in all fairness, the revenues generated by the tax were to be used in the colonies to maintain order and keep peace on the frontier.

The Stamp Act required colonists to pay a tax on every printed piece of paper—newspapers, magazines, broadsides, legal documents such as business licenses, permits, college diplomas, and even playing cards. Most of the fees weren't outrageous, many of them started at less than a half-penny. The devil was in the details. The law required the tax paid in hard currency—gold and silver, which was always in short supply in the colonies. And, the penalties for evading the tax were harsh. The fine was

£10 for each pack of cards or pair of dice sold without a stamp, and £20 for each newspaper or pamphlet that did not list the name and address of the publisher. Tax evaders were to be tried before a Court of Admiralty because Parliament felt colonial juries would be too lenient on tax evaders. The law stipulated counterfeiters would be treated as felons, and suffer the penalty of death without benefit of clergy.

Another thing that riled the colonists was the tax coming so close on the heels of the Currency Act of 1765, and the Sugar Act of 1764 that taxed textiles, wines, sugar, molasses, and coffee.

It wasn't the Stamp Act that bothered the colonists so much, as it was wondering what would come next? In the past, taxes had been levied on the colonies to regulate trade. These new taxes were different. They were passed specifically to generate revenue for the Crown.

Concerned colonists began to ask themselves—if this new tax was allowed to stand, what would the next tax, and the tax after that be?

....

The opposition was immediate, and often violent with two colonies—Virginia and Massachusetts—leading the charge.

The Virginia House of Burgesses lit up with impassioned pleas to remove the tax. Patrick Henry introduced the *Stamp Act Resolves*. The gist of the *Resolves* was the colonists enjoyed the same rights as citizens of Britain. Parliament had no right to tax them. If Virginians were taxed—those taxes should be imposed by rightfully elected representatives from Virginia.

The demand was clear, *no taxation without representation.*

In Boston, the Loyal Nine, the forerunner of the Sons of Liberty spearheaded the protest movement. Members of the group included John

Avery, Henry Bass, Thomas Chase, Stephen Cleverly, Thomas Crafts, Benjamin Edes, Joseph Fields, John Smith, and George Trott.

The Loyal Nine fostered rebellion through mob violence, intimidation, and propaganda. It is likely Samuel Adams wrote many of the articles opposing the Stamp Act that were published by Benjamin Edes in the *Boston Gazette*. The group posted broadsides and pamphlets all around Boston denouncing the Stamp Act. They hung effigies of tax collectors, public officials, and others who supported the tax. They staged their meetings and mob actions from a rallying point at the *Liberty Tree*.

The first public action taken by the Loyal Nine was against Andrew Oliver, the tax collector at Boston. On August 14, 1765, the mob hung Oliver in effigy (a model of him) on Newbury Street, along with a caricature of a boot with the devil climbing out.

Later that evening, the Loyal Nine burned Oliver's property on Kilby Street. With that building still in flames, they made off with the statue of Oliver that had been hung in the tree earlier and headed for his home. Outside of Oliver's house, the mob beheaded the statue of Oliver, while the family watched helplessly from inside. Next, they pelted stones at the house, further terrifying those trapped inside.

After this, the mob proceeded to the Fort Hill District where they burned the headless effigy of Oliver. Most of the crowd gave up and went home at that point, but a few hardcore members egged on by Ebenezer McIntosh, returned to Oliver's (now empty) home, where they proceeded to break out all of the windows and destroy anything of value.

The next day, the Loyal Nine visited Lieutenant Governor Thomas Hutchinson. They demanded he write a letter to Parliament to denounce the Stamp Act. Hutchinson refused. On the night of August 26, a mob took vengeance on his house, looting and destroying the property.

The message was clear—if you supported the Stamp Act, you put yourself at the mercy of the Loyal Nine.

....

Over a very short period, the Loyal Nine morphed into the Sons of Liberty. By the end of 1765, there was a Sons of Liberty Chapter in each of the thirteen colonies, and you guessed it—one of their favorite activities was harassing stamp distributors. Samuel Adams and John Hancock founded the Boston Chapter. Another Boston chapter of the Sons of Liberty, called the *Mechanics,* was formed by Paul Revere. They served as spies, or intelligence gatherers, reporting on the whereabouts of British troops in the city of Boston.

In all fairness, mob violence and intimidation were just a small portion of what the Sons of Liberty were all about. Much of their influence came about through peaceful acts like publishing newspaper articles, pamphlets, and broadsides that lambasted the Stamp Act.

Massachusetts initiated a call for a Stamp Act Congress. Nine of the original thirteen colonies attended the gathering. The Stamp Act Congress met at Federal Hall in New York City in October of 1765 to protest the tax. They issued a *Declaration of Rights* and Grievances which held to the tenant—*no taxation without representation.*

All the fuss came as a complete surprise to members of Parliament. To them, it was a minor tax. None of the money went to the Crown. Every penny of it was to be used to help safeguard the colonies. Prime Minister George Grenville offered to substitute another means of raising revenue if the colonists could suggest a more acceptable one.

British merchants complained about lost profits from colonists protesting the tax. No one was ready to fight a battle over such a piddling amount. Parliament eventually repealed the tax in 1766 because it was cheaper to drop it than to keep it. That same day, Parliament approved the Declaratory Act, which reaffirmed they had "full power and authority to make laws and statutes" over the "colonies and people of America" who were "subjects of the Crown of Great Britain."

. . . .

More than anything else, the Stamp Act crisis paved the way for American independence. It brought the colonies together for the first time when they united to form the Stamp Act Congress. Even more important was the organization of the Sons of Liberty. They would play a pivotal role in every step of the Revolution including the Boston Massacre and the Boston Tea Party.

REAL STORY OF THE BOSTON MASSACRE

Americans have been led to believe the Boston Massacre was just another example of British oppression, and that it was one of the inciting events of the American Revolution.

What if I told you the Boston Massacre wasn't a massacre? Subsequent testimony proved the soldiers fired in self-defense. A group of four street thugs instigated the King Street riot when they attacked several lone British troops.

You'd probably say, "That's not what I learned in kindergarten."

Here's the real story of that fateful day on the Boston Common.

. . . .

Tension ran high in Boston during the winter of 1770. Nearly 4,000 British soldiers occupied the town of 20,000 inhabitants, and occasional clashes with the citizenry were inevitable.

One of the biggest rabble rousers in Boston was a gray-haired old man with a shaky voice and jittery hands. His name was Sam Adams, and if you caught a glimpse of him, you probably wouldn't have given him a second glance. Adams was a seedy, foul-smelling character who went about in dirt spattered clothing. The best way to describe him would be a failure at life. He failed at everything he tried. The only thing he was good at was inciting his fellow Bostonites to take up arms against the British.

Adams didn't much like King George III, he didn't like having British troops stationed in Boston, and if it were up to him, Adams would have called it quits with Britain years before this. He published *The Journal of Events*, a local paper that described fictional atrocities committed by British Soldiers in Boston. The more outlandish and implausible the story the more likely Adams was to publish it.

His followers were called the Sons of Liberty, and many of them were rowdies, street roughs, and other undesirables.

March of 1770 opened with a roar in Boston.

The word around town was the British troops were preparing to attack the populace. On March 4th Bostonians clashed with British soldiers at John Gray's Rope Walk in the Fort Hill District. Mobs roamed the street throughout the night, and into the next day.

March 5th was snowy and cold. By evening that day a foot of snow covered the ground on Boston Common.

Hugh White was the lone guard in the sentry box near the Old State House. A group of boys formed across the street and began lobbing snowballs and insults at the soldier. Their behavior was nothing new to White. The local kids often taunted the guards stationed there.

Suddenly a young boy named Edward Garrick rushed at White. The sentry slugged the boy with the butt of his musket. The crowd began chanting "Kill him! Knock him down!"

White screamed for help as the mob closed in on him.

A giant of a man swung a club nearly breaking White's arm. That was Crispus Attucks. He was the self-proclaimed leader of the mob. Other members of the group included James Caldwell, Samuel Gray, and Patrick Carr. By most accounts, they were street toughs and bullies who enjoyed a good tussle and often amused themselves by terrorizing lone British soldiers.

Captain Thomas Preston and eight soldiers were the first to hear White's desperate screams for help. They raced across the street to help. Testimony from onlookers stated the soldiers "rudely pushed [the crowd] aside, pricking some with their bayonet, and formed in a half circle around the sentry."

The bells of the Old South Meeting House began to chime. In no time the street swarmed with a mob that numbered nearly 100 persons armed with sticks, snowballs, and clubs.

Captain Preston ordered his men to prime and load their rifles. Then he stepped in front of his men to prevent them from firing. For a moment, the guns stayed silent. Voices flared. Snowballs and sticks pelted the soldiers from all directions. Someone cried "fire!" and the soldier's guns spat fire, smoke, and death.

Pandemonium broke loose on King Street.

Crispus Attucks fell dead. Two bullets struck him in the chest, and his warm blood spilled red across the newly fallen snow. Samuel Gray was shot in the head and died instantly. Seventeen-year-old James Caldwell took two musket balls in the back and fell dead in the snow. Patrick Carr took a bullet in the hip. Part of his backbone got blown away as the ball escaped his body. He lingered on suffering immense pain for nine more days. The fifth victim was a boy named Samuel Maverick. He was struck and killed by a musket ball as he made a dash for safety.

Governor Thomas Hutchinson rushed to the scene as soon as he learned of the attack. To prevent further bloodshed, he ordered a special investigation and had Captain Preston and his men arrested.

It was uncertain if the soldiers could get a fair trial in Boston. No lawyers wanted to take the case for fear of being labeled a Tory. Eventually, John Adams and Josiah Quincy signed on as attorneys for the defense. The prosecutor was Robert Treat Paine, a future signer of the Declaration of Independence.

The trial got delayed seven months, and during that time disturbing news leaked out.

Patrick Carr's dying testimony put the kibosh on the massacre theory. Doctor John Jeffries testified about Carr's dying words. On his deathbed, he told Jeffries the four of them—Attucks, Caldwell, Gray, and himself "went with a design against the soldiers, that the soldiers were pelted as they were going to their post, that he thought they were abused and that they really would have fired before…he thought that they fired to defend themselves; that he did not blame the man, whoever he was that shot him; that he blamed himself for having gone to the riot, and might have known better."

Sam Adams was infuriated.

He had been talking up the massacre for months, portraying the soldiers as cold-blooded killers who intended to gun down the innocent citizens of Boston. A color engraving by Paul Revere pictured the soldiers as ruthless killers smiling as they fired into the unarmed crowd.

Captain Preston and six of his soldiers were found innocent and released. Two other soldiers were charged with manslaughter and branded on the thumb.

John Adams would later write, "On that night the formation of American Independence was laid. Not the battle of Lexington or Bunker Hill, not the surrender of Burgoyne or Cornwallis were more important events in American history than the Battle of King Street on 5th March

1770. The death of four or five persons the most obscure and inconsiderable that could have been found upon the continent has never yet been forgiven by any part of America."

Daniel Webster said, "from that moment we may date the severance of the British Empire."

IT'S NOT THE TAX; IT'S THE PRINCIPLE – A SHORT HISTORY OF THE BOSTON TEA PARTY

The Boston Tea Party was a response to British taxes that raised the price of tea in the colonies, right?

Not!

The Tea Act of 1773 reduced the price of tea paid by the colonists. The people hurt by the Tea Act were the smugglers. The lower price of tea undercut their business and ensured the East India Company would have a monopoly on tea.

Here's the scoop.

Because of the three pence tax on tea, colonists boycotted tea from the East India Company, instead favoring smuggled tea and coffee that was cheaper and not subject to the tax. The reduction in sales put the East India Company on hard times. Because of the boycott, the company found itself with sagging profits and an overabundance of tea in its warehouses.

To buoy up the failing East India Company, Parliament passed the Tea Act of 1773. It eliminated the tax on tea charged to the East India Company while at the same time keeping the three pence tax on tea paid by the colonists. It gave the East India Company a virtual monopoly on tea sales in the colonies, that allowed them to undercut the smugglers and still make a good profit.

Another section of the Act, allowed the East India Company to ship their overstock of tea to consignees in the colonies, who would resell the tea to merchants. Forty-five tons of tea arrived at four locations—Boston, Charleston, New York, and Philadelphia.

In each of the cities except Boston, the Sons of Liberty convinced the consignees to resign and forced the ship captains to return to Britain with their cargo. In Boston, Governor Thomas Hutchinson prevented the consignees from resigning. A possible reason for this was two of the consignees were his sons, and one of the others was his nephew. Hutchinson also refused to let the ships leave Boston Harbor without paying the three pence tax on the tea.

Sam Adams, John Hancock, and Joseph Warren led the protest. One of their touch points was *"no taxation without representation."* They considered the three pence tax unconstitutional because the colonies were not represented in Parliament, and thus had no say in imposing the tax.

That was one part of it. The flipside was the Tea Act was bad for business. It shut the smugglers and American merchants out of the trade by favoring the East India Company. Why should the colonies pay taxes, when the Crown eliminated the same taxes for the East India Company?

Given more time things may have worked themselves out, but Boston had a law that required all ships unloaded within twenty days of arriving in the harbor.

The countdown was on.

The Sons of Liberty continued to hold heated meetings protesting the tea. They exhorted Governor Hutchinson to let the ships sail away like they had in New York, Charleston, and Philadelphia. Hutchinson was adamant. He insisted they unload the tea and pay the taxes on it.

The situation came to a head on the twentieth day—December 16th, 1773.

Early that morning nearly 5,000 people gathered outside of Old South Meeting House clamoring for the ships to return to England. A committee formed and went to the customs house. They demanded the ships be allowed to leave the harbor. The Collector of Customs refused to let the ships leave without unloading the tea and paying the tax.

After dark, a group of 150 to 200 men slipped away from the crowd. George Hewes, a participant, said the men covered their faces and hands with coal dust at a local blacksmith shop, then donned Indian costumes. "When we arrived at the wharf, there were three of our number who assumed authority to direct our operations…We then were ordered by our commander to open the hatches and take out all the chests of tea and throw them overboard, and we immediately proceeded to execute his orders, first cutting and splitting the chests with our tomahawks, so as to thoroughly expose them to the effects of the water."

Hewes said the captains of the ships did nothing to stop them. Their only request was that the protestors did not harm their ships or riggings. The British Navy watched but didn't stop them. Hewes said, "We were surrounded by British armed ships, but no attempt was made to stop us."

One of the British officers who watched the Boston Tea Party unfold was Lieutenant-Colonel Alexander Leslie. He wrote Lord Barrington that his men were ready to intervene from their positions at Castle William, but he never received orders.

The British soldiers learned their lesson from the Boston Massacre. They sat back and watched, and waited, as the event unfolded before them. No shots were fired, and no one was injured during the entire three hours it took to dump the tea in Boston Harbor.

The next morning several of the participants returned and noticed undamaged tea floating on the surface of the water. They rowed out to it and beat the tea with their oars to ensure it was unusable. Again, the British did nothing to stop them.

The protestors destroyed nearly two million dollars' worth of tea that night. When word of the Boston Tea Party reached London, Parliament was incensed. As punishment, they passed the Coercive Acts, or Intolerable Acts, that virtually locked down Boston Harbor.

One result was the first Continental Congress was formed to petition the King to repeal the acts.

John Adams wrote, "This destruction of the tea is so bold, so daring, so intrepid and so inflexible, and it must have so important consequences and so lasting that I can't but consider it an epoch in history."

The Boston Gazette reported on December 20, 1773, "The people are universally congratulating each other on this happy event."

It was the first step towards American independence. And, though not a drop of blood was shed, nor a shot fired, a message was sent loud and clear, that a new nation was around the corner.

REAL STORY OF PAUL REVERE

"Listen my friends, and you shall hear of the midnight ride of Paul Revere." Or at least that's how Longfellow's poem begins its telling of the legend of the Revolutionary War hero. The truth is somewhat different.

Two riders set out from Boston that night and were eventually joined by a third. The only catch is none of the three men completed their mission—not on horseback anyway.

. . . .

Paul Revere was a Boston silversmith and sometime spy. He often carried secret messages between Boston, New York, and Philadelphia. So, it's no surprise as the Battles of Lexington and Concord loomed before them that Bostonites recruited Paul Revere to spread the word of the British advance.

On April 16th, 1775, Dr. Joseph Warren dispatched Revere to Lexington to warn Sam Adams and John Hancock the British would soon be on the move. Everyone assumed the target would be the ammunition depot at Concord.

Revere's first ride to Lexington came off without a hitch. On the way back he visited Colonel William Conant in Charlestown, and let him know he would spread the warning when the British troops started to move. The signal he arranged was one if by land, and two if by sea. The signal light was to be hung from the steeple of old North Church.

Two days later on April 18th, some 700 troops under the command of Colonel Francis Smith marched from Boston Common, presumably headed towards Lexington and Concord. Their orders, from General Gage, were to seize and destroy all the ammunition, small arms, and artillery found there.

Gage didn't expect a fight. He assumed the rebels would turn and run at the sight of his troops. After all, what rabble would dare to challenge His Majesty's forces?

As soon as it was determined the British were marching for Concord, Revere headed to old North Church. He instructed Robert Newman, the sexton of North Church, to flash two lights (meaning the British were coming by boat).

After he had lighted the signal lights, Revere set off on his journey.

What most people don't know is a second rider, William Dawes, a young shoemaker from Boston, was dispatched as a backup, in case Revere did not get through. Dawes took the land route where he passed through British troops on the Boston Neck.

Revere rowed across the Charles River where he met Colonel Conant and his waiting troops. After consulting with Conant, Revere borrowed a horse from Deacon John Larkin and began his ride towards Lexington some twelve miles away.

Just after 11:00 PM, Revere passed through a flat marshland known as Charlestown Common. Ahead of him, Revere spotted a British patrol and quickly changed course making his way towards Medford. "In Medford," Revere wrote, "I awaked the Captain of the Minutemen; and after that, I alarmed every house, till I got to Lexington."

Revere met up with the other rider, William Dawes, in Lexington at the home of Reverend Jonas Clark. After grabbing food and refreshments, Revere and Dawes set off together for Concord. Doctor Samuel Prescott joined them en route.

They stopped at every house they came to along the way, and woke the inhabitants shouting, "the regulars are coming."

Midway to Concord, the three riders encountered a British patrol. Prescott and Dawes managed to escape. Revere was captured and held prisoner for a short period. In his account of the incident, Revere says, "I saw four of them [British soldiers], who rode up to me, with their pistols, in their hands, said [goddamn] you stop if you go an inch further, you are a dead man."

When questioned, Revere spilled the beans, telling the British he had been alerting the countryside to their coming. Hard as it is to believe, the British released Revere—a self-confessed spy, less than an hour later.

After his release, Revere made his way back through the fields to Reverend Clark's house in Lexington.

With the British just a few miles behind him, Revere found Adams and Hancock packed and ready to make their getaway. He helped Hancock's secretary hide some of his papers, and made his break for it just as the first shots were fired on Lexington Green.

Thus, ends the "midnight ride of Paul Revere." While he was not entirely successful, the venture was good enough to secure the silversmith his place in history.

WHO REALLY WON THE BATTLE OF BUNKER HILL?

Bostonians received word on June 13th, 1775, that the British were getting ready to fortify some of the smaller hills around Boston, so they could better control access to the harbor. On the night of June 16th, 1775, Colonel William Prescott received orders to fortify nearby Bunker Hill before the British could take control of it.

Prescott marched onto the Charlestown Peninsula that night with 1200 men, and tools, to start the entrenching work. His orders specified he should fortify Bunker Hill. Instead, he decided to fortify nearby Breed's Hill. It was lower and easier to build the redoubts around it. The men worked quietly throughout the night, careful not to betray themselves to the enemy troops close by in Boston Harbor. Prescott slipped away several times to check on the British ships in the harbor. The *Falcon* lay off Moulton's Point; the *Lively* opposite the Navy Yard; the *Somerset* at the ferry; and the *Glasgow* near Craigie's Bridge.

Early on the morning of the June 17th, a sentry on the *Lively* spotted the Americans at work on the redoubt, and the ship opened fire. Shortly after that General Thomas Gage had all the ships in the harbor, along with the batteries on top of Copp's Hill, open fire on the American entrenchments.

The British commanders formed a council of war to decide their next move. General Henry Clinton favored a siege, whereby they could starve the rebels out with little loss of life on either side. Generals Howe and Burgoyne pressed for an immediate attack, saying the American troops were "rabble" who could not stand up to the King's troops.

The British rowed across the harbor in longboats. General Howe and 1500 men landed near Moulton's point. After scouting out the enemy position, Howe requested reinforcements from Gage. His troops settled in, relaxed, and ate lunch while they waited. Howe's reinforcements arrived about 2:00 PM. Another group landed near the eastern edge of Breed's Hill, at Madlin's Shipyard (the Navy Yard).

While General Pigot's troops waited outside of Charlestown, snipers inside the city harassed and killed many of his men. The battery on Copp's Hill lobbed a round of incendiary shot into the village square, and flames roared through the town center. Admiral Graves sent a detachment of marines from the *Somerset* to fire the eastern part of the town, and flames soon engulfed the entire city.

Howe's troops marched forward, four deep, coming at the colonial troops like sheep going to slaughter. The British carried full packs that weighed upwards of 100 pounds while trying to jump fences, maneuver through tall grass, and make their way through overwhelming heat. The Americans watched, and waited, heeding Colonel Prescott's command, not to fire "until you see the whites of their eyes."

General Howe stayed in the thick of the battle and urged his men to keep up the fight. Two of his aides were shot down beside him. "Three times" he was left in the field "by himself, so numerous were the killed and wounded about him." His men gave way, and retreated, many making a wild dash for the boats.

Shortly after that, Howe rallied his troops and led them back over the same path, only this time they were forced to march over their dead and dying comrades. An American in the redoubt observed, "It was surprising to see how they would step over their dead, as though they had been logs of wood." This attack was even more deadly than the first. The colonial troops were lined up in three columns, ensuring there was always someone with a gun loaded, and ready to fire. The regulars fell like flies. And yet, they kept coming.

Eventually unnerved by the rebel fire, the Regulars broke ranks and retreated towards the waterfront. Howe and his officers tried to rally them with no success.

For a moment, it seemed as if the battle was over. The Americans watched and waited. Their powder supply was almost gone. Prescott had his men break open the remaining artillery shot and distributed what little powder they could gather. The men who had bayonets guarded the points, where they expected the British would scale the breastworks.

When it came time to make his third attack, Howe ordered his men to strip off their cumbersome knapsacks and to hold their fire. Howe led the remainder of the grenadiers and light infantry in a frontal assault on the breastworks. Generals Clinton and Pigot moved on the extreme left, where they were to scale the redoubt. British artillery raked the redoubt and the area by the rail fence. The regulars marched up Breed's Hill. Their orders were to deploy for a bayonet charge when they were within fifty yards.

The Americans opened fire, taking down as many of the regulars as they could, but their powder soon ran out. The British stormed the redoubt from every direction. The fighting was soon hand-to-hand. Bayonet against musket butt.

After intense fighting, the Americans retreated across Bunker Hill, leaving over 100 dead on the field. The British casualties were over 200 dead, and 800 wounded—making it one of the largest losses they would suffer during the entire war.

Once the fighting ended, many questions remained unanswered.

There was no pressing need for either side to take possession of the hill that day. The British commanded the harbor. General Clinton's plan to lay siege to the defenders on Breed's Hill would have brought the matter to a quick end. The Colonials had no food or water so they could have only held out for a short period.

The Americans messed up just as badly. The decision to build their defensive works on Breed's Hill, instead of Bunker Hill, left them vulnerable to British attack. Breed's Hill was lower and easier for the British to scale. Bunker Hill was taller, and almost impossible for an offensive force to mount, making it nearly impregnable. In effect, the Colonists were doomed from the start, because the entrenching party disobeyed orders, and made a poor choice of which hill to fortify.

But, the bigger problem was the issue of command. Some commanders disobeyed orders, especially during the third charge, and kept their men on Bunker Hill, rather than sending them to help defend the redoubt. Because of this, Colonel Prescott was forced to order a general retreat.

WHO CREATED THE FIRST FLAG? BETSY ROSS, GEORGE WASHINGTON, OR FRANCIS HOPKINSON?

Betsy Ross is as American as mom, apple pie, and Chevrolet, but is she for real? What would you say if I told you 99.9 percent of Americans never heard of Betsy Ross before 1870?

It's true.

Elizabeth Ross was an obscure Philadelphia upholsterer, and sometimes flag maker, until her grandson, William Canby presented a paper before the Pennsylvania Historical Society in 1870. The nation was gearing up for the bicentennial celebration when Canby decided to share his grandmother's story with the world. And, it was just what the country needed at that time—a female hero.

As it turned out, Betsy Ross wasn't just a flag maker. She was a storyteller, as well. And, the story she shared with her children, and grandchildren, was a whopper they would never forget.

Here's the story as Canby told it.

Somewhere between May 23rd and June 7th, 1777, three members of the Congressional Flag Committee visited Betsy Ross in her upholstery shop on Arch Street in Philadelphia. The committee members included George Washington, Robert Morris, and Colonel George Ross (a member of the Continental Congress, and an uncle of her late husband).

The three men were on a mission to create the new nation's first official flag. George Washington himself asked Betsy Ross to make it. The committee already had a design in mind and showed it to Betsy to get her input.

Canby said, Betsy replied "she could try," but first she had a few suggestions to make it even better. The original design was unsymmetrical, so Betsy suggested a few changes, the most important of which was to use a five-pointed star instead of the six-pointed star designated by the Committee. When questioned about the difficulty of making a five-pointed star, Betsy grabbed her shears, and quickly cut it out.

The Committee was impressed and retired to a back room of the upholstery shop to mull over the new design. George Washington himself took charge and sketched the new design, taking pains to get it just right.

When Washington finished drawing the new flag the members of the Committee hurried off to have a local artist, William Barrett, make a painting as a guide for Betsy. Betsy scurried off to visit a local warship so she could examine the ship's colors.

As soon as the painting was finished, the Committee members brought it back to Betsy, and she quickly made the new flag. It was accepted the next day, and Colonel Ross gave Betsy one hundred pounds to get started making all the colors she could crank out.

So far, so good. The only problem is—there's no evidence to support the story.

For something so newsworthy, there is no coverage of the story in the local or national press. On June 14, 1777, there is a short one sentence reference to the flag on page 235 of Dunlap's *Journal of Congress*. "Resolved that the flag of the United States be thirteen stripes alternately red and white; that the Union be thirteen stars in a blue field representing a new constellation."

Further research by Canby placed George Washington, Robert Morris, and Colonel George Ross in Philadelphia at the stated time. The only thing missing is hard evidence. Nothing points to Betsy Ross as the first flag maker. The journals of the Continental Congress don't have any record of a Flag Committee. There are no receipts payable to Betsy Ross. Canby counters with the claim Congress often formed as many as six committees a day, most of which went unrecorded. As further evidence, he says that amidst the turmoil and fighting during that period, making a flag would have been considered trivial, and not worth mentioning.

Finally, lacking real evidence, Canby included affidavits from Betsy Ross's daughters, granddaughters, and nieces reciting stories they heard as children.

In truth, it's a great story—one we all learn in elementary school, but one that very likely will never be proven.

Betsy Ross's personal story was just as remarkable.

She was born Elizabeth Griscom on January 1st, 1752. She was the eighth of seventeen siblings and apprenticed to William Webster as an upholsterer. Betsy met her first husband John Ross while working for Webster. They eloped in 1773 when she was twenty-one. John Ross was a soldier in the Continental army and died in 1776 from injuries he incurred during an accidental gunpowder explosion on the Philadelphia waterfront.

A year later she married Joseph Ashburn, a sailor in the Continental Navy. His ship got captured in 1781, and he died the next year in a British prison. She married again in 1783 to John Claypoole. That union lasted thirty-four years until he died of natural causes in 1817.

Betsy Ross lived until 1836, sharing stories of her adventures with her children, grandchildren, and neighbors.

. . . .

The other claimant to designing the first flag is Francis Hopkinson.

He was born into a wealthy family, graduated from the College of Philadelphia, and went on to become an author, musician, and customs collector. In 1761 he hung out his shingle as a lawyer. Hopkinson was a New Jersey delegate to the Continental Congress, and one of the fifty-six signers of the Declaration of Independence.

After the Revolutionary War, Hopkinson served as a member of the Constitutional Convention. In 1789 George Washington appointed him a U-S District Judge for Pennsylvania.

He was a consultant to the Great Seal Committee in 1776 and helped to design the Great Seal of the United States. In 1778 Hopkinson created a fifty-dollar Continental currency note, and later a forty-dollar note.

His claim to creating the American flag stems from an invoice he submitted to Congress in 1780. They rejected it because he didn't include any vouchers to back up his expenses.

Like Betsy Ross there is no hard evidence to support Hopkinson's claim as a designer of the first American flag.

YORKTOWN – FINAL BATTLE OF THE REVOLUTION

Fortune smiled on George Washington.

On the morning of August 14, 1781, he received a dispatch from Admiral de Grasse that he was moving his fleet from its station in the West Indies to the Chesapeake Bay. At about the same time, Washington received word from Marquis de Lafayette that he had Lord Cornwallis' army bottled up at Yorktown.

Washington's mind reeled with the possibilities. He'd waited six long years for this opportunity. Victory was finally within his grasp. Water surrounded Yorktown on three sides. The only way out was through a narrow strip of land patrolled by the Marquis de Lafayette. Without knowing it, Cornwallis had marched his army into a trap, and Washington intended to spring it.

If, he could move fast enough.

On August 19th, Washington, Rochambeau, and a force of 6,000 men—2,000 Continental troops, and 4,000 French soldiers started their march south. The column stretched out for nearly two miles, and what a spectacle the ragtag army must have made as it marched through Philadelphia and Virginia. The Continental troops wearing their battered homespun uniforms marched at the head of the column, followed by the French in their fancy new uniforms. To spectators, it must have appeared as if the French had captured the Continentals, and were marching them off in disgrace.

On September 5th, Washington and Rochambeau rendezvoused with the French fleet at the head of the Chesapeake Bay and made sail for a spot near Yorktown. Lafayette positioned his men on the neck of land at Williamsburg on September 7th, cutting off any hope Cornwallis had of making a retreat.

Count de Grasse arrived in the Chesapeake Bay on the 13th with 26 ships of the line. Washington reached Lafayette's headquarters on the 14th. By the 20th the rest of his men filtered in, and Washington possessed a force of 16,000 to Cornwallis' 7,000.

On October 11th Cornwallis wrote General Henry Clinton, "On the evening of the ninth their batteries opened and have since continued firing without intermission...We have lost about seventy men, and many of our works are considerably damaged. [We] cannot hope to make a very long resistance." On the 12th he added, "We continue to lose men very fast."

The cannonading continued throughout the 13th and 14th. Lafayette's Light Infantry charged the redoubt nearest the river. Colonel Alexander Hamilton and Colonel Henry Laurens charged the redoubts on the flanks.

On the 15th Cornwallis's message to Henry Clinton was desperate. It expressed his concern defeat was close at hand. "The safety of this place is therefore so precarious that I cannot recommend that the fleet and army should run great risk in endeavoring to save us."

On the night of the 16th, Cornwallis attempted a last ditch effort to escape. Sixteen boats set sail after dark. A handful of soldiers stayed behind to surrender the city. Unfortunately, the weather turned, and a violent storm appeared out of nowhere, driving many of the boats down the river.

Escape was impossible.

Cornwallis surrendered the next day. Ironically, the British fleet sailed out of New York with a relief party bound for Yorktown that same day. When he received news of the garrisons' capitulation, Clinton returned his fleet to New York. The Americans took sixteen-thousand British soldiers prisoner, 156 died in the fighting, and 326 were wounded. The American losses numbered 72 dead, and 180 injured.

The British marched out of Yorktown as their regimental band played the tune, *"The World Turned Upside Down."*

She be damned, says the farmer, and do her he goes
First roars in her ears, then tweaks her old nose,
Hello Goody, what ails you? Wake woman, I say,
I am come to make peace in this desperate fray.
Derry down, down, hey derry down,
I am come to make peace in this desperate fray.

Alas, cries the old woman, And must I comply?
I'd rather submit than the hussy should die.
Pooh, prithee, be quiet, be friends and agree,
You must surely be right if you're guided by me,
Derry down, down, hey derry down,
You must surely be right if you're guided by me.

The war would continued for several more years in other theaters, but no more major battles would be fought in North America. News of the surrender reached England in November of 1781. Some say George vowed to continue the fight, but Parliament, like most of the English people had had enough. On February 17, 1782, Parliament voted to cease hostilities and seek peace with the colonies.

The final peace was made on September 3, 1783, when the two nations signed the Treaty of Paris. Shortly after that on November 25, 1783, the last British troops sailed out of New York.

After eight long years of fighting and struggle freedom was at hand.

REVOLUTIONARY WAR TO CIVIL WAR

If the Revolutionary period created America as a free and independent nation, the period from the American Revolution to the Civil War helped define what the new nation would become.

Four years after the end of the Revolution the states recognized the Confederation wasn't working. Just as he led the country through the war years, George Washington guided the nation through the Constitutional Convention. Beginning in 1785 Washington worked behind the scenes with James Madison, and some of his other advisers from the Revolution, to craft a new government. When the Convention met in 1787, George Washington was unanimously elected President of the Constitutional Convention, and the reason most states ratified the Constitution was they expected George Washington to be the leader of the new government.

Washington assumed the Presidency in 1789 and faced the challenge of guiding a new nation. One of the first major crises he faced was the Whiskey Insurrection. To pay off its Revolutionary War debt, Congress levied a tax on distilled spirits in 1791. From the start, backwoodsman in four rural counties in western Pennsylvania rebelled against the tax, threatening tax collectors, and refusing to pay. Washington eventually marched 13,000 men to the area of the insurrection, and put down the rebellion. His handling of the crisis set an important precedent that the government could use the militia to enforce laws. Andrew Jackson used the threat of military force to put down the South Carolina Nullifiers in 1832. Abraham Lincoln used the same rationale to justify calling out troops during the Civil War.

Thomas Jefferson's signing of the Louisiana Purchase in 1804 moved the nation one step closer to reaching from coast-to-coast. One of Jefferson's greatest accomplishments as President was sending Lewis and Clark, and Zebulon Pike to explore the new territories. They returned with a wealth of information about the new area, and the native tribes that whetted everyone's desire to learn more.

In 1812 the United States fought a second war of Independence with Great Britain. Among the many reasons for the war were British impressment of American sailors into the Royal Navy and British support of Indian tribes against settlers on the Western frontier. America won the war, but none of the original issues were resolved. So, the question remains who won that war?

After Andrew Jackson took the helm in 1828, the Northern States became more industrialized. Factories sprouted up throughout the north; the first railroad tracks were laid, and a new political party—the Democrats, took hold. Jackson weathered the National Bank crisis, put down one of the first significant challenges to the Constitution—the South Carolina Nullifiers, and began the policy of Indian Removal. The Black Hawk War cleared the way for settlers to move into Iowa, and the rush to the West was on.

James K. Polk engineered the Mexican War, and in so doing completed Jefferson's dream of extending the nation from coast-to-coast. The Treaty of Guadalupe Hildago signed in 1848 officially ended the war, and set the American border in Texas at the Rio Grande, and gave America possession of California, New Mexico, Arizona, Nevada, Utah, and parts of Wyoming, and Colorado. In return, America paid Mexico $15 million dollars and agreed to settle certain war claims.

REMAKING THE GOVERNMENT

As early as 1784, it was apparent to George Washington, James Madison, Alexander Hamilton, and other politicians the new government wasn't working. The government under the Articles of Confederation was weak. It didn't have the necessary powers to raise taxes, and police disputes among the thirteen states.

One of the first attempts to rework the Articles of Confederation was the Annapolis Convention held in 1786. A group of five states—New York, New Jersey, Pennsylvania, Delaware, and Virginia, got together to determine what they could do to rework the Confederation. One major outcome of the meeting was the call for a broader Constitutional Convention to be held in Philadelphia the next year.

Meanwhile, George Washington, James Madison, Alexander Hamilton, and Henry Knox worked behind the scenes from Mount Vernon to draft a new Constitution. James Madison was the primary architect of what would become known as the Virginia Plan. It laid out a vision for the new government that included a strong central government, a bicameral legislative system (that included the House and Senate), and an executive, and legislative branch.

The Constitutional Convention was held at Independence Hall in Philadelphia from May 14 – September 17, 1787. George Washington was unanimously elected president of the Convention. He wore his military uniform and presided over it—sitting in a tall chair, on a raised platform overlooking the other delegates.

From the outset, Madison's Virginia Plan was the starting point for the new Constitution. Virginia Governor Edmund Randolph presented it to the Convention.

As the first order of business, the delegates decided to work behind a veil of secrecy. They sealed the windows and doors and stationed guards inside and outside of Independence Hall. Nothing was to be spoken, or printed, about what happened during the Convention. George Mason explained to his son, the reason for meeting in secrecy was because things aren't always what they appear to be. People may have gotten the wrong idea about the new Constitution if they only knew partial details about the debates. By waiting until the Convention ended before releasing any details about the document, Americans could examine the new Constitution in its entirety.

One sticking point was the executive office. Some representatives worried a strong executive might attempt to seize power. Many delegates favored a committee of three, rather than having just one executive officer who exercised unlimited power. Alexander Hamilton preferred a president appointed for a lifetime term. George Mason proposed a single executive who would rule for seven years, with no opportunity of reelection. John Rutledge made the final recommendation in August, suggesting the president is elected by the House of Representatives using a system of electoral votes.

Many delegates worried about empowering a strong executive. The only reason they acquiesced was because everyone expected George Washington would become the first president.

Another issue that plagued the Convention was the apportionment of representatives for the new government. The smaller states worried because they felt they were underrepresented in the new government. Rhode Island refused to participate because they were afraid of losing their rights. The Southern states worried because the northern states had a larger population. They were concerned that would give them more say in the new government. The final compromise counted slaves as three-fifths of a person to apportion representation. The decision gave the Southern states more representation in the House of Representatives and the Electoral College.

Slavery was another ugly issued that raised its head during the Constitutional Convention. James Madison would later write, the real difference between the states was not size—big or small, but between northern and southern states. Ninety percent of the nation's slaves lived in the states of the South, and Southerners relied upon slave labor to run their plantations. In the north, many states had already banned slavery. Their economy was more industrialized and did not rely on slave labor.

Even slaveholders were ambivalent, and unsure what to do about slavery. Edmund Randolph was a large slaveholder, but he would have abolished slavery if he could have. Thomas Jefferson and George Washington suffered from the same ambivalence. They were unsure how to justify owning slaves, while at the same time advocating individual freedoms.

The final decision on slavery came down to economics. In return for a twenty-year ban on restricting the Atlantic slave trade, the south removed a provision in the Constitution that required all goods be shipped on American vessels. That was good for the northern economy, and the delegates reluctantly agreed to the compromise.

Because of this, the slavery issue took a twenty-year hiatus. Most delegates realized they were leaving a smoking gun for future generations, but it was the only way they could broker a deal that worked for both the north and the south.

. . . .

Delegates ratified the Constitution on March 4th, 1789. George Washington was sworn in as the first president of the new nation on April 30th. Over the next eight years, he would craft a new government, creating the cabinet system, and developing many of the departments we are familiar with today.

WHISKEY INSURRECTION – AMERICA'S FIRST ORGANIZED REBELLION

The *Whiskey Insurrection* was the first test of the Federal Government's right to impose and collect taxes, and to call out the militia to enforce those laws.

Farmers in western Pennsylvania tottered on the edge of rebellion during the early 1790s. The Whiskey Tax threatened their livelihood. Eastern and Western Pennsylvania, were separated by an almost insurmountable barrier called the Allegheny Mountains. The market west of the Alleghenies was limited. To sell their grains east of the mountains, growers had to load their crops on pack horses and transport them across dangerous mountain terrain. The problem was twofold: 1) Grains were difficult to transport, and a tough sell once they got them across the mountains. 2) Whiskey was easier to transport, and easier to sell.

Because of this, numerous stills operated in Western Pennsylvania, transforming grain into whiskey.

In 1791 Congress passed a tax on distilled liquors. It based the fees charged to the capacity of a brewer's still, rather than the spirits produced, and it required the tax paid in cash. That put small producers at a disadvantage. Western Pennsylvania distillers produced less whiskey.

Because of that they paid a larger tax per gallon than Eastern distillers, who could increase their whiskey production and cut the tax, they paid per gallon. The other sticking point was the law required the tax to be paid in cash. Barter was the currency of the western frontier. Most distillers paid their bills in whiskey—not cash.

The law required still owners to register with the government. If they violated the law or refused to register and pay taxes, they were required to stand trial in a Federal court, some three hundred miles away in Philadelphia. The result was a long and costly journey few grain farmers could afford.

Protests spread through the western territories. The farmers held a meeting at Redstone Fort on July 27th, 1791. Representatives met in each of the four respective western Pennsylvania counties—Washington, Westmoreland, Fayette, and Allegheny.

Most westerners took the easiest course of action and refused to pay the tax.

Excise offices were supposed to be set up in each county to collect the taxes. The rebel's response mimicked the tactics used by the Sons of Liberty during the American Revolution. Federal collectors were threatened, tarred and feathered, and tortured. People who offered space for tax collectors to set up their offices suffered the same fate as the tax collectors.

A new reign of terror began in 1793 as insurrectionists shot up the stills of their neighbors who complied and paid the fees. Many small distillers were damned if they did, and damned if they didn't. One such incident happened in Allegheny County where the rebels destroyed William Cochran's still.

Federal Marshal David Lennox was dispatched to the area in July of 1794 to serve arrest warrants to protestors who refused to pay the tax. Revenue officer John Neville accompanied Lennox as he served the writs.

They served a warrant on William Miller on July 15th. As they were leaving Miller's home, an armed mob began shooting at them. On July 16th, the mob attacked Neville's house. Neville and his slaves exchanged gunfire with the rebels, and one of the rebels, Oliver Miller, was killed during the battle. Protestors faded away after Miller's death, but later that day a mob of nearly 500 local militia converged on Neville's house.

Luckily for Neville, a force of ten Federal soldiers from Fort Pitt came to his rescue and helped him escape. The rebel leader, James McFarlane, was killed in the fighting. Neville's house and outbuildings were burned down. Gunfire from the mob increased, and the outnumbered soldiers eventually surrendered.

In Fayette County, rebels burned the home of the tax collector, Benjamin Wells. The biggest protest occurred at Braddock's Field, just outside of Pittsburgh, in July of 1794. Thousands of protestors met there to determine a course of action on how to fight the tax.

A delegation consisting of Attorney General William Bradford, Pennsylvania Senator John Ross, and Pennsylvania Supreme Court Justice Jasper Yeates conferred with the rebels in late August and early September of 1794. The delegation returned to Philadelphia on September 24th and reported military action would be required to resolve the problem.

George Washington decided it was time to stop pussy-footing around. He called out the militia from several states. On September 19th, 1794, he joined a force of 12,950 men gathered at Carlyle, Pennsylvania. Washington marched as far as Fort Cumberland, Maryland with the troops, then turned control of them over to General Henry "Light Horse" Lee, and Secretary of the Treasury, Alexander Hamilton.

By mid-November, the militia had rounded up and arrested nearly 150 men suspected of taking part in the Whiskey Rebellion. Twenty men were eventually taken to Philadelphia to stand trial. Officials convicted two men for treason. By the start of December, most of the army returned home. Fifteen hundred troops stayed behind to police the frontier.

George Washington was satisfied with the results. The invading force didn't kill a single person. Some individual rights were tromped on in making the arrests, but the government's power to levy taxes was secure, as was its right to use the military to enforce laws.

The Whiskey Insurrection established the right of the Federal government to use the military to enforce unpopular laws and to preserve the Union. Andrew Jackson would use the same tactics during the South Carolina Nullification Crisis in 1832. Abraham Lincoln would use them again to preserve the Union during the Civil War.

ANDREW JACKSON - PRESIDENT, SOLDIER, AND BIGAMIST

Andrew Jackson was a man possessed by demons. He had the temper of a saltwater crocodile, was fiercely independent, and quick to pull a gun when angered. History tells us he was a man of the people, but one thing is sure, Jackson lived his life like he was destined for greatness.

Andrew Jackson was born in the Waxhaw settlements of the Carolinas in 1767. He served as a courier in the Revolutionary War and was taken prisoner at age thirteen. A British officer slashed him across the face with his saber for refusing to polish his boots. He wore the scar from that incident for the remainder of his life.

Albert Gallatin described Jackson as "a tall, lank uncouth-looking personage with long locks of hair hanging over his face." Thomas Jefferson said, "His passions are terrible…he was Senator, and he could never speak on account of the rashness of his feelings." Marie Emily Donelson Wilcox described Jackson like this. "Tall, angular, reddish bristling hair, face badly freckled and pock-marked, he was awkward and constrained, unattractive in person and repulsive in manner."

Of course, how you saw Jackson depended upon the mood you found him in, and he was a man of many moods. To women, children, and his slaves, Jackson was helpful and compassionate. To his enemies and those who crossed him, the general was ruthless. His one saying that best described him was, "to the victor go the spoils." If you were unfortunate enough to tangle with Jackson, the best advice was to get out of his way.

Andrew Jackson met the love of his life shortly after he moved to Tennessee. Her name was Rachel Donelson Robards. By all accounts, she was a real beauty. One of her relatives wrote, she "had a sweet oval face rippling with smiles and dimples and bright with intelligence—just the style of beauty irresistible to Jackson's type."

At the time, Jackson, and his friend Judge Overton boarded in a cabin owned by Rachel's mother, Mrs. John Donelson. Rachel and her mother lived in the cabin next door, and the two soon struck up a friendship.

Rachel had recently separated from her husband, Lewis Robards. Rachel said, Robards had a violent temper and was physically abusive. Lewis Robards said the couple had been experiencing temporary marital difficulties. When he came back to claim his wife, he found her cavorting with Andrew Jackson.

Robards applied to the Legislature of Virginia for a divorce on December 20th, 1790. As grounds for divorce, he stated Rachel had committed adultery with Andrew Jackson. Fearing Robards might come after her and drag Rachel off with him, the couple made their way to Natchez, Mississippi, where they got married in the spring of 1791.

During a 1793 visit to Jonesborough, Jackson learned the divorce wasn't finalized until September 27th, 1793. Shortly after that, Andrew Jackson and Rachel Robards re-said their vows before a justice of the peace. That was on January 18th, 1794.

That ended the story for thirty-four years. It was something the couple could joke about with friends and family over a jug of corn whiskey or a pipe of tobacco until the presidential campaign of 1828 raised its nasty head. Unfortunately for Jackson, and John Quincy Adams, that campaign opened a whole new can of worms in electioneering. Political mudslinging, dirty tricks, and outlandish accusations became the new norm in politicking.

No one knows for sure who started it.

Bad feelings lingered from the campaign of 1824. Andrew Jackson was sure John Quincy Adams and Henry Clay stole the election from him. Jackson won the popular vote, but political maneuvering by Henry Clay cost him the election. Jacksonians called it the "corrupt bargain." In return for delivering Adams the presidency, Henry Clay became Secretary of State, a position that at the time was considered a stepping-stone to the presidency.

From that point on Jackson made it his business to build the alliances he needed to win the election in 1828.

Political slurs circulated fast and loose on both sides. Jackson's supporters accused John Quincy Adams of having premarital sex with his wife, pimping out his chambermaid to the Czar of Russia while he was the Russian Ambassador, and keeping gambling devices in the White House. The opposition said Adams purchased a billiards table and chessboard with public funds.

There were so many incidents to use against Jackson; it's hard to determine exactly where to begin. Jackson's violent temper and fierce independence had helped him so much in his rise to power and greatness, but it gave his enemies unlimited fuel to use against him.

The worst part of it for Jackson were the accusations leveled against his family. The opposition said Jackson's mother was a filthy whore who prostituted herself to the British during the Revolution, and his beloved Rachel a bigamist and adulteress. They accused Jackson of being an adulterer and stealing another man's wife. As soon as Jackson won the election, many newspapers proclaimed Rachel "unfit to be allowed in the White House."

Philadelphia printer John Binns issued what was called the "coffin handbill." It pictured six black coffins that referred to Jackson's actions in the War of 1812 when he ordered the execution of six soldiers for desertion.

Jackson won the election by a landslide. However, what should have been a happy time for the old general turned sour. Rachel died suddenly, just before Christmas in 1828. Jackson buried her in the old garden of the Hermitage on Christmas Eve.

Andrew Jackson was heartbroken.

The doctors said Rachel died of a heart attack. Andrew Jackson wasn't so sure. He blamed her death on John Quincy Adams, and the smear campaign his people ran against her. When he arrived in Washington Jackson refused to visit the outgoing president. For his part, John Quincy Adams left town before Jackson's inauguration and refused to pass the torch to the incoming president.

Such is politics.

ANDREW JACKSON VERSUS THE SOUTH CAROLINA NULLIFIERS

Here's another story from the Jacksonian era that isn't as well-known as it should be. The South Carolina Nullification Congress of 1832 was a harbinger of things to come.

The question was if a state disagrees with federal law, does it have the right to nullify it, and disregard that law? Vice-president John C. Calhoun argued state's rights superseded federal statutes. President Andrew Jackson believed to his dying day that Calhoun was a damned traitor and that he should have strung him up from the nearest branch.

Here's a quick overview of the nullification crisis, the events leading up to it, and its eventual outcome.

Since the War of 1812, Congress had imposed a series of protective tariffs Southern states felt favored Northern manufacturers. The Tariff of 1828 raised the cost of British textiles, making it more attractive for people to purchase American cloth. The problem for Southern states was just the opposite. The tariff shrunk the English demand for cotton. Because of this, their economies suffered.

South Carolina felt the tariff was unfair and damaged their economy. When Andrew Jackson was reelected president in 1832, South Carolinians expected he would lower the tariff significantly. When the new tariff of 1832 passed with only minimal changes, South Carolina decided it was time to shake things up a bit.

. . . .

The American economy experienced a slowdown through much of the 1820's. During the final days of John Quincy Adams' administration, the government passed the Tariff of 1828. The idea behind the tax was to encourage people to *buy American* by making foreign cloths and materials more expensive.

South Carolina felt the taxes targeted them particularly hard. One of the reasons behind this was the increasing industrialization of the northern economy, while the South remained primarily agrarian, relying upon the plantation system, and slave labor to power its economy. During that period, nearly 60,000 white residents fled the state searching for better pickings elsewhere.

The three key players in the Nullification Crisis were: Andrew Jackson, John C. Calhoun, and Henry Clay.

John C. Calhoun served as vice president under John Quincy Adams. When he sensed a change in the political climate, Calhoun switched allegiances and became Andrew Jackson's vice presidential running mate in the 1828 election. Unbeknownst to Jackson, Calhoun penned *The South Carolina Exposition*. The pamphlet challenged the Tariff of 1828, especially, the constitutionality of a protective tariff. Calhoun's interpretation of the constitution was that tariffs could be levied only for revenue related reasons, nothing else.

Calhoun initially kept his authorship of *The South Carolina Exposition* secret, because like other southerners he anticipated Jackson would repeal the tariffs. When that didn't happen, a riff developed between the two men. Calhoun eventually resigned the vice presidency on July 14th, 1832. He decided to run for the Senate in South Carolina, where he felt he could do more to support the nullification issue.

Calhoun was a strong state's rights advocate. He believed states had a right to nullify federal laws that went against their best interests—and even to secede from the Union. Andrew Jackson thought just the opposite. In a *Proclamation* published on December 10th, 1832, Jackson wrote, "*I consider, then, the power to annul a law of the United States assumed by one state incompatible with the existence of the Union, controlled expressly by the letter of the Constitution, unauthorized by its spirit, inconsistent with every principle on which it was founded, and destructive of the great object for which it was formed.*"

South Carolina called for a Nullification Convention in November of 1832. In it, they proclaimed the Tariffs of 1828, and 1832, unconstitutional and therefore null and void in that state. The convention set a deadline of February 1st, 1833, after which they would no longer enforce the laws within their borders.

Andrew Jackson considered three possible responses to the nullification crisis:

- Do nothing, and essentially agree states had the right to override Federal laws that were not to their liking.
- Affect a compromise to placate South Carolina and prevent the ensuing crisis.

- Pull a George Washington. In 1794 when a group of Pennsylvanians refused to pay the newly enacted whiskey tax Washington didn't waste any time showing the rebels he meant business. He marched 12,950 troops to Pennsylvania and put the rebellion down without firing a single shot.

Seven small naval vessels and a man-of-war sailed for Charleston in November of 1832. General Winfield Scott readied the army. Governor Robert Hayne of South Carolina drilled 25,000 militia men, preparing them to resist the anticipated onslaught of Federal troops.

For a short period, armed conflict seemed inevitable.

Andrew Jackson submitted the *Force Bill* to Congress on January 16th, 1833. If passed, it would have closed the customs houses at Georgetown and Beaufort, and set them up on ships in those harbors. They planned to move the Charleston Customs House to Castle Pinckney or Fort Moultrie. The bill would have allowed the United States to use military force to collect the tariffs.

On January 21st, South Carolina postponed the nullification deadline—in hopes a compromise could be worked out. At the same time, Henry Clay jumped in and brokered a compromise bill. It promised to reduce the tariff in small increments back to twenty percent by 1842. The South Carolina Nullification Convention reconvened and overturned the nullification ordinance on March 11th, 1833.

The crisis was averted, and the nation returned to business as usual.

The real issue—un-talked about at the time, but understood by everyone—was slavery. It went without saying: If the Federal government could impose economic restrictions that went against a state's best interests—they could also outlaw slavery, and with it—the Southern way of life.

Many historians contend Andrew Jackson's response to the nullifiers was too mild. Had he followed his initial reaction to march United States troops to South Carolina, put down the rebellion, and hang John C. Calhoun as a traitor, there may never have been a Civil War.

BLACK HAWK AND THE FIRST INDIAN WAR WEST OF THE MISSISSIPPI RIVER

The Black Hawk War was the first Indian war fought west of the Mississippi River. The only thing is by the account of most participants it wasn't a war. It was more of a massacre.

Of course, we all know the telling of history is all about which side you're on. The story of the Black Hawk War is no different. It was a mix-up of frontier madness, mayhem, and murder. Illinois Governor John Reynolds called out the militia and raised thousands of volunteer troops. General Winfield Scott marched his Regulars half way across the country to Fort Armstrong, at Rock Island. Lieutenant Colonel Zachary Taylor led a group of infantrymen in the fighting.

Every yokel and backwoods frontiersmen with a grudge against the Indians joined the fray. A slew of future presidents, congressman, senators, and military leaders launched their careers on the Indian's misfortune.

Abraham Lincoln served as a frontier ranger and spy. Two years later he began his political career as an Illinois Congressman. Zachary Taylor served in the heat of several battles. Later he was a hero of the Mexican War, and soon after that President of the United States. Winfield Scott distinguished himself in the War of 1812. After the Black Hawk War, he negotiated treaties with several Indian tribes that ceded over sixty million acres of land to the United States. He earned more fame in the Mexican War, and in 1852 he ran unsuccessfully for President on the Whig ticket. Jefferson Davis was on furlough for most of the war but returned in time to escort the prisoner Black Hawk down the river to Jefferson Barracks at St. Louis. During the Civil War, he served as President of the Confederacy.

Several opportunities presented themselves to end the conflict without spilling any blood. Instead, they were bungled.

The first chance to end the campaign peacefully had come before a single shot was fired. Another opportunity to end the war presented itself just before the battle of Bad Axe. Black Hawk attempted to hail Captain Throckmorton onboard the steamboat Warrior. American troops disregarded the Indian's flag of truce and fired upon them. What followed over the next few days was the massacre of nearly seven hundred men, women, and children of the Sac tribe.

What's remarkable about the Black Hawk War is it set the tone for future conflicts between the whites and the Indians in the opening of the American West. The land was set aside exclusively, by treaty, for the use of the Indians. As pioneers moved further westward, they encroached upon the Indian lands, building homes, and fencing in their lands. When the Indians complained to authorities, their concerns went unanswered.

During the troubles that followed, the settlers beat or killed some of the Indians who got in their way. When the Indians retaliated, the frontier went into a panic, and troops rushed in to save the day. Frontier troopers attacked and pushed the Indians further westward when by treaty, they were obligated to protect the Indian lands from the white settlers who were squatted on them.

On November 3rd, 1804, the United States government concluded a treaty with the Sac and Fox Indians. By the terms of this treaty, the Indians ceded fifty million acres of land. Article 7 of the treaty — became one of the chief causes of the Black Hawk War. It stipulated that, "as long as the lands which are now ceded to the United States remain their property the Indians belonging to the said tribes shall enjoy the privilege of living or hunting upon them."

The last portion of the treaty became the sticking point. If the Sac had been forced to leave their lands as soon as they ceded it to the government, there would have been no problem. Instead, they continued to occupy the land for nearly thirty years. Black Hawk's memory grew fuzzy. He insisted his people never sold the land his village was on.

On April 6th, 1832, Black Hawk, five hundred warriors, and their squaws and children, crossed the Mississippi at the Yellow Banks, below the mouth of the Rock River, and advanced into the state of Illinois. News of the Indian invasion spread like wild-fire throughout the settlements. Those settlers who didn't join the militia made their way to the larger settlements where they built crude stockade forts. Inside the forts, the settlers formed themselves into garrisons and prepared for the impending Indian attacks

The first engagement was a comedy of errors. Major Isaiah Stillman bivouacked his troops in a clump of open timber, three miles southwest of the mouth of Sycamore Creek while his men scouted the area trying to find Black Hawk's warriors.

Black Hawk says he had decided to surrender. Therefore, when he learned Stillman's troops were nearby, he sent three of his braves to make peace. They walked towards the soldiers carrying a white flag of truce. Five other braves followed at a safe distance so they could keep Black Hawk informed of what was happening. A group of cavalry spotted the five watchers and chased after them. Two of the five braves died in the pursuit. The other three escaped and made their way back to Black Hawk, telling him that two of their number died along with the three flag-bearers.

After he learned what happened to his messengers, Black Hawk gave up all thoughts of surrender. He tore up his flag of truce and encouraged his men to attack the soldiers, despite the fact they were outnumbered and faced almost certain death.

What should have been a peaceful end to the Black Hawk War turned into a full-fledged tragedy for whites, and Indians alike. Black Hawk said, "I was forced into war, with about five hundred warriors, to contend against three or four thousand."

Black Hawk and the Sacs vanished into the wilderness moving their band towards Wisconsin.

After dusk (several months later) a large party of Indians, composed mainly of women, children, and old men, were placed on a large raft and in canoes. Black Hawk hoped the soldiers at Fort Crawford who guarded the mouth of the Wisconsin River, would allow these noncombatants to cross the Mississippi in peace.

He was wrong.

Lieutenant Ritner opened fired on the canoes a short distance above Fort Crawford. Fifteen men died in the attack, thirty-two women, and children, and four men were captured. Close to that number drowned as they tried to escape. Of those who made it to the woods, all but twenty died of hunger or were massacred by a party of Menomonee led by Colonel Stambaugh.

That was the Battle of Wisconsin Heights.

On the night before the final battle, the Sacs attempted to surrender again. Towards the middle of the afternoon the steamboat *Warrior*, commanded by Captain John Throckmorton arrived.

As the steamer neared the shore, Black Hawk stepped onto the bank holding a white flag. He called out to Captain Throckmorton in Winnebago requesting him to send a boat ashore so the Sacs could give themselves up. A Winnebago traveling on the *Warrior* told Throckmorton Black Hawk wished to surrender, but the Captain was suspicious.

The Battle of Bad Axe was later described as a "slaughter," by many of the soldiers who fought in the campaign. Historian Reuben Gold Thwaites wrote, "Some of the [Sacs] succeeded in swimming to the west bank of the Mississippi, but many were drowned on the way, or coolly picked off by sharpshooters, who exercised no more mercy towards squaws and children than they did towards braves — treating them all as though they were rats instead of human beings."

Governor Reynolds of Illinois wrote, "Some squaws were killed by mistake in the battle. They were mixed with the warriors and some of them dressed like the males."

Another participant in the battle, John Wakefield wrote, "It was a horrid sight to witness little children, wounded and suffering the most excruciating pain."

In the end, nearly one thousand Sacs gave their lives fighting a war none of them chose to make. After the battle, Black Hawk was taken, prisoner. Later he was sent to Washington, where he met with President Andrew Jackson. The War Department took him on a whirlwind tour of east coast cities to convince him how foolhardy it was to fight the White Man.

Upon his return home, Black Hawk lived a peaceful life. He visited many of the old-time settlers, and towards the end of his life, he participated in several Fourth of July parades.

The words he uttered to Andrew Jackson are as poignant today as they were then. "I am one man. You are another."

INDIAN REMOVAL, AND THE TRAIL OF TEARS

One of the most vexing problems facing Americans in the 1820s and 1830s was what to do with the Native Americans. In the north, the Indians were pushed further westward with the advance of civilization. In the south, the advance of population served to bottle the Indians up. They were constrained by the Atlantic Ocean and the Gulf of Mexico. There was nowhere for them to go except to new lands in the west.

One result of this was Indian removal.

The Southeast was home to the Five Civilized Tribes—the Cherokee, Creek, Choctaw, Chickasaw, and Seminole. Settlers were hungry for the Indian lands. Even though a treaty-protected much of it, neither the states nor the army could protect the Indians from greedy settlers who wanted their lands.

To land-hungry Americans, the Native Americans were standing in the way of progress. The natives didn't plant crops, or develop their property, so the settlers figured they didn't have any real claim to it.

During the period from 1814 to 1824 numerous treaties were made with the tribes to exchange Indian lands in the east for new lands in the west. The problem was very few Indians took advantage of the opportunity.

The Five Civilized Tribes attempted to assimilate into white culture. They became farmers and purchased slaves to work their lands. The Cherokee adopted a legal constitution in 1827 that declared they were a "sovereign nation," just like the treaties said they were. The state of Georgia refused to recognize them. The Supreme Court concurred.

The Cherokee challenged the ruling. The Supreme Court agreed they possessed the right to self-government, but Georgia refused to accept the decision. Andrew Jackson said, "Mr. Marshall has made his decision. Now let him enforce it."

Late in 1827, just over 700 Creeks began their journey to Fort Gibson, Indian Territory. Over the next year, 1600 more Creeks made the trip west. They arrived in September of 1829 amidst a cholera epidemic. When they saw the conditions that waited for them in Indian Territory many of the new arrivals turned around and headed back to Alabama.

Andrew Jackson pushed the Indian Removal Act through Congress in 1830. It allowed the president power to negotiate treaties to remove the Indian tribes to lands west of the Mississippi. For those Indians who decided to stay, they were to become citizens of the state they lived in. The intention of the act was voluntary and peaceful removal.

Instead, Jackson used the act to force Indian removal.

The Choctaws agreed to remove from their lands in 1830. Things didn't go well for the tribesmen who decided to stay. The government did a poor job of protecting them from encroachment by squatters who wanted their land. The whites stole their cattle, destroyed their crops, and constantly harassed them. Most of the Choctaws eventually packed up and left, deciding things couldn't be any worse in the west.

The Seminoles decided to fight it out. They engaged in the First Seminole War in 1817 – 1818. Some tribe members signed a treaty in 1833 agreeing to removal, but most stayed. They wound up fighting in a Second Seminole War that spanned the period from 1835 – 1842. That was followed by the Third Seminole War from 1855 – 1858. The government eventually paid the remaining tribesmen to leave rather than fight again.

The Creeks took a different path. The tribe signed a treaty agreeing to give up some of their lands in exchange for the right to stay. Once again, the government couldn't, or wouldn't, protect them from encroaching settlers. In 1836 the government forced 15,000 Creeks to remove from their lands without signing a treaty.

Authorities tricked the Cherokee into the removing. In 1833 a treaty was signed with a few tribe members who weren't recognized as tribal leaders. The tribe petitioned the Supreme Court to have the treaty overturned, but in 1836 the court ratified the treaty. The government gave the tribe two more years to move west on their own. If they didn't, they promised to use force to remove them.

By 1838 less than 2,000 Cherokee had removed to Indian Territory. President Martin Van Buren sent General Winfield Scott and 7,000 United States troops to remove them forcibly. Scott's troops rounded the Cherokee up like cattle, at the point of a bayonet, and locked them in stockades until they could affect removal. The tribesmen were not allowed to gather any of their possessions. Instead, they were forced to watch squatters move in, and loot, and destroy their homes.

After being rounded up like animals, the Cherokee were forced to march to their new homes in Indian Territory. At least 3,500 of their tribesmen died on what was dubbed the "Trail of Tears." The marchers suffered from whooping cough, typhus, cholera, and starvation. Many of the soldiers who escorted the Cherokee couldn't believe the conditions the natives endured. They said the Cherokee suffered more than anything they experienced during the Civil War years later.

For Andrew Jackson and Martin Van Buren, Indian Removal was a success. Nearly 50,000 Native Americans were removed from the southern states, and over 25 million acres of land was opened to white settlers.

STEALING THE SOUTHWEST – JAMES K. POLK AND THE MEXICAN WAR

As students, we're taught to believe America is always on the side

of right, and would never start a war just to steal land from another country, right?

It's an interesting thought, but history doesn't quite bear it out.

....

James K. Polk was probably the most unsociable, drab, stick-in-the-mud ever to be elected president. Fun was a four-letter word in his book. Sports, drinking, dancing, anything to do with being around people didn't make his A-list. He was short, scholarly, lived for his work, and avoided face-to-face conversations and confrontations whenever possible.

About the only thing, Polk had going for him was his friendship with Andrew Jackson. Jackson's support pushed Polk into the White House. And, the general made sure Polk understood the two key goals of his presidency were to annex Texas and Oregon.

Four years, a war, and several treaties later Polk would accomplish it all.

....

After Texas won its independence from Mexico in 1836 most citizens of the Lone Star State favored annexation by the United States. Americans weren't as sure about the idea. President Martin Van Buren worried the move could trigger a war with Mexico. Both, the Democrats and Whigs, worried it could cause a split in Congress over slavery in the new territory. Annexation was a moot point until President John Tyler raised the issue in 1844.

The Senate voted annexation down in June of 1844. Tyler brought the issue before Congress again in early 1845. This time it passed on March 1st, and Texas joined the Union as a state on December 29th.

In the fall of 1845, President Polk offered Mexico five-million dollars if they would recognize the Southwestern Boundary of Texas at the Rio Grande. He offered another five-million-dollars for New Mexico, which at that time included parts of Nevada and Utah. Polk also made a twenty-five million dollar offer for California. When Mexico refused his offers, Polk decided to force the issue. He sent General Zachary Taylor and 3,000 troops to Corpus Christi, Texas. In March of 1846, General Taylor moved his troops into the disputed territory between the Rio Grande and Nueces Rivers.

About a month later a detachment of Mexican Cavalry crossed into the disputed territory and engaged in a minor scuffle with a small force of American soldiers. Polk used the attack as an opportunity to declare war on Mexico. His proclamation issued on May 11th said, "Mexico…invaded our territory and shed American blood upon the American soil." Two days later Congress approved Polk's declaration of war.

The *New York Daily Tribune* published an editorial on May 15th, 1846. It said, "Three months ago, if a party of our people had gone down to the Rio Grande, halted opposite of Matamoros, threatened that city with cannon, and blocked the River, they would have been marauders and land pirates, and everybody would have admitted that Mexico was justified in so treating them."

They followed those words up declaring "...our troops and not Mexicans, are the actual and wrongful invaders."

Congressman Abraham Lincoln protested the war demanding Polk should identify the "exact spot" where the Mexican Army "shed American blood upon the American soil."

It was evident to almost everyone; the United States provoked Mexico into a war it was trying hard to avoid. Even today Mexico labels what we call the Mexican War, *The United States Invasion of Mexico.*

Polk's excuse for sending troops was a promise he made to protect Texas after its annexation. He ordered the army to prepare for war, positioned naval vessels near American ports, and sent General Taylor with 3,000 troops to Corpus Christi, Texas. His thinking was it would be a short war, with just a few minor engagements. Then he would resume negotiations for the land purchases he desired.

As it turned out the war lasted two years, cost over one hundred million dollars, and claimed the lives of nearly thirteen thousand Americans.

The Treaty of Guadalupe Hidalgo that ended the war. It required the United States to pay Mexico fifteen million dollars and settle a little over three-million dollars in claims of American citizens against Mexico. In return, the border with Texas was set at the Rio Grande, and the United States received California, New Mexico, Nevada, Wyoming, Utah, and Colorado. The area was complimented by the Gadsen Purchase in 1853 - 1854. America purchased portions of Arizona and New Mexico for ten million dollars.

Under the auspices of the Mexican War, the United States stole or purchased (depending on how you look at it), nearly one-third of Mexico's land. For the first time, the country stretched from the Atlantic to the Pacific coast.

The one downside was its effect on the slavery issue.

Congressman David Wilmot tried to add a provision to an appropriations bill on August 8, 1846, that would have outlawed slavery or involuntary servitude in areas acquired through the Mexican conflict. The *Wilmot Proviso*, as it came to be known, was hotly contested by Southern states and failed to pass. Wilmot tried to revive it in 1847, and again in 1848 when he tacked the measure onto the Treaty of Guadalupe Hidalgo.

CIVIL WAR

The Civil War didn't come as a surprise to anyone. The Founding Father's had an inkling it was coming as early as the Constitutional Convention, but they skirted the issue of slavery, leaving it for future generations to resolve.

South Carolina Senator James Chestnut, Jr. resigned from the Senate on November 10th, 1860, four days after Abraham Lincoln's election as President. President James Buchanan delivered a message to Congress on December 3rd, in which he stated he believed secession was unconstitutional, but at the same time, he didn't think the government had the legal right to stop a state from seceding. Buchanan's message angered Southerners because it said secession was illegal, and it angered Northerners because he didn't do anything to try to stop it.

South Carolina seceded from the Union on December 20th, 1860. By the time of Lincoln's inauguration on March 4th, 1861, six more states had joined South Carolina in seceding from the Union. All the while James Buchanan sat quietly in the White House, refusing to do anything to hold the Union together.

So, the question was—Could James Buchanan have prevented the Civil War?

Command was a major problem for Abraham Lincoln during the first years of the war. His generals were indecisive and refused to go into battle. The few times they fought decisive actions, such as Antietam and Gettysburg, they failed to follow up, and press their advantage.

General McClellan was a thorn in Lincoln's side from day one. He spent his first six months as commander in chief of the army training and readying his troops. Lincoln waited what seemed like an eternity until he began to call the Army of the Potomac "McClellan's Bodyguard." After McClellan's victory at Antietam, Lincoln was stunned McClellan didn't chase down Lee's troops and fight another battle.

Not long after this, the army went through a series of command shakeups until George G. Meade was appointed commander in chief. Three days later Meade's army met Robert E. Lee at Gettysburg to fight the bloodiest battle of the Civil War. When it was over more than 50,000 men lay dead on the battlefield. Lincoln was grateful for the victory, but disappointed Meade didn't press his advantage, and fight another battle.

John Wilkes Booth was the George Clooney of his day. At age twenty-six he was one of the most successful actors on the stage earning $500,000 in 2015 money. But, Booth had a dark side. He was a Southern supporter and despised Abraham Lincoln for starting the war.

Sometime in 1864, the wheels in Booth's head began to churn. He rounded up a gang of like-minded conspirators and started piecing together a plot to kidnap Lincoln. Booth's plan was to grab Lincoln near the Soldier's Home outside of Washington, spirit him into the South, and ransom him for a favorable settlement to the war. As time passed, and the war neared its end, Booth pieced together a desperate plan to kill Lincoln, General Grant, Secretary Seward, and vice president Andrew Johnson.

After assassinating Lincoln, Booth escaped into Maryland and Virginia leading Government forces on a two-week chase. Federal troops cornered him at Richard Garrett's farm, near Bowling Green, where he was shot and killed.

Just days before the assassination, General Robert E. Lee surrendered to General Ulysses S. Grant at Appomattox Court House.

The war was over.

COULD JAMES BUCHANAN HAVE PREVENTED THE CIVIL WAR?

Many historians say James Buchanan was a "weak, timid, old man" who didn't do anything to prevent the Southern states from seceding. Some historians, have even gone so far, as to declare Buchanan was an "accessory after the fact." He was a president, Southern sympathizer, and a traitor.

But, was he?

The obvious comparisons are Andrew Jackson and George Washington. Andrew Jackson stood firm during the South Carolina nullification crisis and threatened to kick the nullifiers in the ass and hang all the traitors from the nearest tree branch if they laid a single hand on Federal property or fortifications. During the Whiskey Insurrection, George Washington marched 13,000 troops to western Pennsylvania to put down the insurrection.

James Buchanan, by comparison, hid away in the White House and issued this message to Congress on January 8th, 1861. "No state has a right by its own act to secede from the Union or throw off its Federal obligations at pleasure…" However, he continued, "To [Congress] belongs the power to declare war, or authorize the employment of military force…"

In effect, he said, *I'm president, and secession is illegal, but I don't have any power to act or stop the individual states from seceding. It's up to Congress.*

That's a wimpy response, at best.

To better understand it, we need to take a deeper look at Buchanan's presidency. Just days after his inauguration, the Supreme Court handed down the Dred Scott decision which stated that African Americans, whether freemen or slaves, had no standing to sue in Federal courts. Moreover, it said Congress had no authority to regulate slavery in states or territories acquired after the formation of the United States.

Buchanan was sure the Dred Scott decision had settled the slavery issue once and for all. Instead, Northerners worried the decision would cause slavery to be legalized in the newly organized Western states, and then possibly restored in the northern states. For the South, it was a vindication that slavery was legal, and strengthened their belief abolitionists were enemies of the Union.

Tensions continued to flare throughout Buchanan's presidency. In 1857 he supported the Lecompton Constitution, a document that would have protected the rights of slaveholders in Kansas. Northern Democrats, notably Stephen Douglass (architect of the Kansas-Nebraska Act), were outraged by the document. One result was the split in the Democratic Party during the 1860 election that enabled Abraham Lincoln to win the presidency.

Perhaps the biggest problem was Buchanan's failure to make a stand— for, or against, slavery. He continued to hold that slavery was a constitutional issue, not one the executive could decide. He said: "The Constitution…expressly recognizes the right to hold slaves as property in states where slavery exists. This, then, is not a question of general morality affecting the consciences of men, but it is a question of Constitutional law."

And, after that, "...our Union rests upon public opinion, and can never be cemented by the blood of its citizens shed in civil war...Congress possesses many means of preserving it by conciliation, but the sword was not placed in their hands to preserve it by force."

The final break came on December 20th, 1860. South Carolina passed the Ordinance of Secession and formally seceded from the Union. Five days later, Howell Cobb, Secretary of the Treasury stepped down, because Buchanan said secession was illegal. Shortly after that, Lewis Cass, Buchanan's Secretary of State, resigned because he didn't feel the president was doing enough to stop secession.

Between January 9th and February 1st, 1861, six more states seceded from the Union—Mississippi, Florida, Alabama, Georgia, Louisiana, and Texas.

In January of 1861, Senators Stephen Douglass and William Seward attempted to placate the Southern States. When that failed, Virginia led the call for a Peace Convention. It was held at Willard's Hotel in Washington and was presided over by the former president, John Tyler. At the end of the conference in mid-February, several proposals that would have required new amendments to the Constitution were delivered to Congress. They were reviewed in committee and set aside.

Of course, there is another possible explanation for Buchanan's inaction. Perhaps he was waiting for the South to strike the first blow. It would have been much easier to sell a war to Congress, and the people, if the South was the aggressor. That's what happened with Lincoln.

Abraham Lincoln was inaugurated on March 4th. In early April, President Lincoln advised South Carolina Governor, Francis Pickens he was going to send supplies to Fort Sumter. The Confederate Government ordered Major Anderson, the commander of Fort Sumter to evacuate the fort. He refused. Confederate troops attacked Federal forces at Fort Sumter on April 12th, and Anderson surrendered the fort on the 14th.

On April 15th, 1861, Abraham Lincoln issued a proclamation calling for 75,000 troops to help put down the rebellion.

The Civil War had begun.

DISASTER AT BULL RUN, ORGANIZING FOR WAR

Bull Run was the first major battle of the Civil War.

It was a total defeat for the Union. Early in the day, they had the advantage, but by late afternoon the Confederates received reinforcements, and Federal troops were forced to retreat. They fled the battlefield, discarding their weapons, as they made a wild dash back towards Washington.

The Confederate troops could have won the rebellion then and there but lacked the discipline and organization necessary to press their advantage.

Several days later, President Lincoln and Secretary Seward visited the battlefield. General Sherman said, "Mr. Lincoln stood up in the carriage, and made one of the neatest, best, and most feeling addresses I ever listened to, referring to our late disaster at Bull Run, the high duties that devolved on us, and the brighter days yet to come."

One outcome of the battle was Abraham Lincoln realized he was in for a long fight. Any hopes he had for a quick victory disappeared. General George P. McClellan replaced General Irvin McDowell as commander of the army.

Lincoln described the position he was into A. G. Riddle. "I am the President of one part of this divided country at least, but look at me! I wish I had never been born! I've a white elephant on my hands, one hard to manage. With a fire in my front and rear, having to contend with the jealousies of the military commanders, and not receiving that cordial cooperation and support from Congress that could reasonably be expected, with an active and formidable enemy in the field threatening the very lifeblood of the Government, my position is anything but a bed of roses."

The Mason and Slidell scandal rocked the nation in November of 1861. Mason and Slidell were Southern politicians who had been sent to England to seek recognition of the Confederacy. They were traveling on the British Steamer "Trent" when the United States Steamer "San Jacinto" captured them. Great Britain violently protested the search and seizure of her ship. For a short time, war with England appeared imminent. Secretary Seward worked out an amicable solution whereby the two prisoners were released, and the crisis blew over.

By the winter of 1862, Lincoln had a million men in the field. Unfortunately, he didn't have a single general willing to fight a battle.

General John C. Fremont assumed command of the Western army in the summer of 1861. On August 30th, he stunned Lincoln, and the entire nation when he issued a proclamation that stated any citizen of Missouri who took up arms against the United States would have their property seized and their slaves declared freemen.

Fremont surrounded himself with his supporters and refused to go into battle. Lincoln sent General Curtis with orders to remove Fremont. The order included one stipulation. If Curtis discovered any evidence Fremont had fought a battle or was about to fight one, he should not remove Fremont.

General David Hunter replaced Fremont.

Since the start of the war, General George McClellan had proven himself to be a thorn in Lincoln's side. Lincoln waited patiently for

McClellan to build and train his army. After he accomplished that, Lincoln expected him to go into battle, but McClellan hesitated so much Lincoln began calling the Army of the Potomac, "McClellan's bodyguard." For his part, the general showed outright contempt for Lincoln. On more than one occasion, he refused to receive Lincoln when he visited his camp.

On September 17th, McClellan overtook Lee's army at Antietam and defeated him. Instead of following up his victory, and chasing after Lee's retreating army, McClellan stayed in camp.

Lincoln became frustrated with McClellan's inaction and visited him on the battlefield.

What he found was, McClellan, surrounded by 100,000 men, once again acting as his personal bodyguard. Lincoln surveyed the camp. He interviewed McClellan's generals, visited wounded soldiers in the makeshift hospitals, and talked with soldiers in the field. The next day he returned to Washington and sent McClellan the following order, "The President directs that you cross the Potomac and give battle to the enemy or drive him south."

A week later, McClellan and his troops had not budged. Lincoln wrote him again, "You remember my speaking to you of what I called your over-cautiousness? Are you not over-cautious when you assume that you cannot do what the enemy is constantly doing?"

McClellan responded his "cavalry horses had sore tongues."

Lincoln telegraphed back, "I have just read your dispatch about sore-tongued and fatigued horses. Will you pardon me for asking what the horses of your army have done since the Battle of Antietam that fatigues anything?"

On the first of November, Lincoln gave up all hope of McClellan taking to the field and removed him from command of the army.

General Ambrose Burnside was appointed the commander of the Grand Army of the Republic. Shortly after that, he engaged Lee's forces at Fredericksburg. The results were disastrous. More than ten thousand Union soldiers perished in the battle.

BATTLE OF GETTYSBURG

The Battle of Gettysburg was a major turning point for the Union army.

In late June of 1863, Confederate General Robert E. Lee led a 75,000-man force into Pennsylvania. Among the areas threatened by this invasion were Philadelphia, Baltimore, and Washington.

On the eve of this threat, the Commander of the Union Army, Fighting Joe Hooker, resigned his commission and was replaced by General George G. Meade. Three days after accepting the command, Meade engaged Lee's forces at Gettysburg.

On June 30th, General John Buford's cavalry held Oak Ridge and McPherson's Ridge, just west, and north of Gettysburg. Advance scouts for his army spotted Confederate forces outside of Gettysburg on the Chambersburg Pike. The battle commenced early on the morning of July 1st. By late afternoon 19,000 Federal troops faced 24,000 Confederates. Union troops retreated through the city as they found themselves outnumbered. Newspapers reported, "Rebel sharpshooters are very troublesome shooting at our men from the steeples of churches."

Towards the end of the day reinforcements arrived. General Meade's troops formed a fishhook-shaped line that stretched across Culp's Hill, Cemetery Hill, Cemetery Ridge, and Little Round Top. At the end of the day, it appeared to be a Confederate victory. Robert E. Lee's troops held the city and formed a six-mile-long position around the Union forces.

The second day of the battle saw some of the heaviest fighting at Little Round Top, Culp's Hill, and Cemetery Hill. Massive losses occurred on both sides as the Union troops held their positions. *The Raftsman's Journal* (July 15, 1863) wrote, "During the second day the Rebels fought with a desperation never witnessed before, but finally toward evening they were driven back at every point..."

Early in the day, Lee ordered an all-out assault on Union forces dug in just south of the town. General Longstreet massed 10,000 men near Little Round Top as he readied for battle. Union troops rushed to the position. Colonel Joshua Chamberlain, a former professor at Bowdoin College, was ordered to hold his position at all costs. Chamberlain fought off one charge after another and then had his men fix their bayonets for a desperate charge down Little Round Top. The shocked Confederate troops turned and ran; many others dropped their guns and surrendered on the spot.

By the end of day two, there were 35,000 dead on the field at Gettysburg.

On the third day of the battle, July 3rd, General Lee planned a massive attack on Meade's center. In the morning, the Confederate infantry retreated from their position on Culp's Hill. At 1:00 the Rebels began a massive artillery bombardment. General E. P. Alexander later wrote, "The two signal guns were heard in quick succession. In another minute, every gun was at work. The enemy were not slow in coming back at us, and the grand roar of nearly the whole artillery of both armies burst in on the silence…The enemies position seemed to have broken out with guns everywhere, and from Round Top to Cemetery Hill was blazing like a volcano. The air seemed full of missiles from every direction."

"It seemed madness to launch infantry into that fire, with nearly three-quarters of a mile to go in the midday July sun." As quickly as it started, the cannonading stopped. Alexander sent word to Pickett that it was now or never. If he waited any longer, he would not have enough ammunition left to support him. General Longstreet thought the charge was a mistake and tried to stop Pickett, but it was too late.

"Pickett's division swept out of the wood and showed the full length of its gray ranks and shining bayonets." Fifteen thousand men raced across the mile-long distance to Cemetery Ridge. The infantry no sooner started its charge when the Federal artillery resumed its fire. "A terrific infantry fire was now opened upon Pickett, and a considerable force of the enemy moved out to attack the right flank of his line. We halted, unlimbered, and opened fire upon it. Pickett's men never halted." They swarmed forward, letting loose a barrage of gunfire, as they charged the enemy line, and "were swallowed up in smoke—and that was the last of them."

Alexander said, "the conflict hardly seemed to last five minutes before they melted away." Seven thousand men lay wounded and dead after less than a half-hour of fighting.

Lee's army was forced to retreat in furious battle. One newspaper wrote, "On Friday night…Lee took advantage of the darkness to retreat…and was in full flight on Saturday."

On July 4th, Meade telegraphed General Halleck, "We now hold Gettysburg. The enemy have abandoned a large number of their killed and wounded on the field."

It was a major victory for the Union Army, but Abraham Lincoln couldn't but think Meade had missed an opportunity to put a swift end to the war. Soon after the battle, Lincoln wrote, "Now don't misunderstand me, I am profoundly grateful down to the bottom of my boots for what he did at Gettysburg, but I think that if I had been General Meade, I would have fought another battle."

JOHN WILKES BOOTH

Imagine what it would be like to wake up, flip on the morning news, and discover Bradley Cooper, or Ashton Kutcher, had assassinated President Obama at the movie theater. That's what happened on the morning of April 15th, 1865. People were shocked when they learned John Wilkes Booth had killed President Lincoln.

Booth was one of the most famous actors of his day. He was young, just twenty-six years old, considered one of the most attractive men in America. He stood five feet, 8 inches tall, had a lean, athletic build, ivory skin, and curly, jet black hair. Booth had a reputation as a lady's man, and women mobbed him, on and off stage.

At the time, he killed Lincoln, Booth was pulling down $20,000 a year as an actor (that's roughly half a million dollars in 2015 money). And, yet—he sacrificed it all for his political beliefs.

What was going on in the mind of John Wilkes Booth? What was it that turned this mild-mannered actor into one of the most hated men of his generation?

....

Booth came from a dynasty of thespians.

His father, Junius Brutus Booth, was considered one of the finest Shakespearian actors of his day. He was over-fond of drink, prone to spells

113

of near madness, and according to one source, Junius Booth penned a letter to President Andrew Jackson in 1835, threatening to kill him, unless he released two pirates.

John and his brothers, Edwin, and Junius, Jr. were stage favorites. John never won the acclaim his brother Edwin did but given time; many critics feel he could have outperformed him.

Booth made his acting debut in 1855, at the age of seventeen, as the Earl of Richmond in Shakespeare's *Richard III*. He was good, but not great. There's some evidence he often forgot his lines or missed cues, but the girls liked him anyway. His looks compared to a young Sinatra or Elvis.

He joined the Know Nothing Party (a white supremacist group that wanted to limit foreign immigrants) in the 1850s. In 1859 he enlisted in the Richmond Grays, a Virginia Militia unit that helped put down John Brown's abolitionist uprising at Harper's Ferry. After Brown's capture, Booth stood guard by the scaffold during Brown's hanging.

Booth's acting career exploded after he engaged Matthew Canning, a Philadelphia lawyer, as his agent. He opened his professional career playing Richard III in Montgomery, Alabama. George Alfred Townsend wrote, "His conception of Richard was vivid and original, one of the best we have had."

He soon appeared in venues all over the country including—New York, Chicago, Baltimore, Boston, Washington, St. Louis, and Richmond. He was best known as a Shakespearian actor starring in Romeo & Juliet, Hamlet, Macbeth, and the Merchant of Venice. Booth made his New York Stage debut in 1862. The *New York Herald* reported he was a "veritable sensation." The Washington Intelligencer said his Romeo was "the most satisfactory of all renderings of that fine character." Abraham Lincoln was in the audience at Ford's Theater on November 9, 1863, when Booth played Raphael in *The Marble Heart*.

....

There was no doubt; Booth was a successful actor, a handsome young man, and a Southern sympathizer. The question is: Why didn't John Wilkes Booth just join the Confederate army? What was the trigger that made him jump from Southern sympathizer to presidential assassin?

Part of it was an outgrowth of his political beliefs. The Know Nothing Party was a White Supremacist group that wanted to limit immigration, especially of the Catholics and the Irish. It's known Booth supported slavery, and was against freeing blacks. In a letter to his brother-in-law in November of 1864, Booth proclaimed, "This country was formed for the white, not the black man."

Booth was arrested in St. Louis, in 1862, for making anti-Union remarks. It was no secret he despised Lincoln and blamed him for the South's problems. In 1864 Booth began recruiting agents to help him carry out a plot he devised to kidnap Abraham Lincoln. Booth's original plan was to kidnap Lincoln on one of his many rides to the Soldier's Home outside of Washington. Once they captured him, the conspirators were going to transport Lincoln to Richmond, where the South could ransom him to end the war on their terms, or to facilitate the exchange of captured Confederate soldiers.

There is some evidence to suggest Booth was working with the Confederate government to kidnap Lincoln, but no substantial proof exists. In 1864 he met with Confederate sympathizers at Parker House in Boston, and again in October of 1864, he stayed at St. Lawrence Hall in Montreal, Canada, a known rendezvous for the Confederate Secret Service.

In November of 1864, the conspirators began meeting at Mary Surratt's boarding house in Washington. Members of the group included—David Herold, George Atzerodt, John Surratt, and Lewis Payne.

On March 17th, 1865, the conspirators learned Lincoln would be attending the play, *Still Waters Run Deep*, near the Soldier's Home. Unfortunately, for Booth, Lincoln changed his plans at the last moment and ended up attending an event at the National Hotel in Washington.

Robert E. Lee surrendered to General Ulysses S. Grant on April 9th, 1865. Two days later Booth was in the audience listening to an impromptu speech Lincoln gave at the White House. After he listened to Lincoln talk about giving limited Negro Suffrage, Booth told David Herold, "That means nigger citizenship."

If there was one decisive moment where John Wilkes Booth's plans changed and moved from kidnap to murder, that was it.

THEY'VE KILLED THE PRESIDENT

The Presidential Party arrived at Ford's Theater around 8:30 PM.

William Withers, Jr., the orchestra leader, said they played "Hail to the Chief" as the Lincoln's entered the theater. The crowd stood up and cheered for the President. They waved handkerchiefs and hats to salute him. As Lincoln entered the Presidential Box, he smiled down at the audience and bowed to the crowd before sitting down.

The President sat in a rocker close to the balcony. Mrs. Lincoln sat in an armchair next to him. Miss Harris was at the far right, and just behind her, Major Rathbone had a seat on the sofa.

Booth paced the sidewalk outside of Ford's Theater just before 10:00 PM. He enjoyed a brandy at an adjoining saloon and walked slowly towards the theater. He asked John Buckingham, the doorman, for the time, and made his way towards the stairs. He passed around the dress circle, moving towards the door leading to the President's Box. William Withers, Jr. saw Booth walking on the balcony, moving towards the President's Box, but didn't think anything about it because Booth was a regular visitor to the theater.

Lincoln's bodyguard that night was John Parker, a Washington, D.C. policeman. Parker guarded the little passageway outside of the entrance to the Presidential Box. He abandoned his post several times during the performance; once to watch the play from the first gallery. After the intermission, he disappeared altogether with Lincoln's footman and coachman to visit a nearby tavern.

Because of this, the Presidential Box was left unattended.

Booth crept in through the unguarded door. After entering the passageway, he grabbed a block of wood and barred the doorway shut. Chances are he took a moment to steady himself as he peered into the President's Box.

At 10:20 PM Booth crept through the door with his Derringer raised and leveled. He fired a ball into the back of President Lincoln's head. Lincoln slumped forward, motionless.

Inside the box, white smoke from the powder and shot formed a cloud making it hard to tell what happened. Mary Lincoln screeched. Major Henry A. Rathbone jumped to his feet and began to struggle with Booth. Booth lashed out with his dagger. He thrust at Rathbone's heart. Rathbone blocked the blow with his arm. The knife dug several inches deep into his arm and tore into his chest.

Booth broke free. Rathbone grasped at Booth's coat but didn't have the strength to hold him. Booth jumped to the stage, catching his leg in the draped flags as he leaped.

Wither's testimony gives a vivid account of what followed.

I "heard the crack of a revolver," as I returned to the orchestra. "I saw a man jump from the President's Box onto the stage. He ran directly to the door leading to the backstage. This course brought him right in my pathway. He had a dagger in his hand, and he waved it threateningly. He

118

slashed at me, and the knife cut through my coat, vest, and underclothing. He struck again, the point of the weapon penetrating the back of my neck, and the blow brought me to the floor. I recognized him as J. Wilkes Booth, and watched him make his exit to the alley."

Another witness to the assassination, a Miss Porterfield, was attending the play with her mother. She told her story in a 1913 issue of *Century Magazine*. "We heard the report of a pistol shot, followed almost immediately by Booth's dramatic leap from the President's Box. I remember distinctly the gleam of his dagger as he descended to the stage. I heard him shout something ... I could not clearly distinguish his words, of course later they were [known] "sic semper tyrannis!" "The South is avenged!"

"Looking up to the box, I could not see the President, but I could see Mrs. Lincoln and hear her shrieks and moans."

In confusion, most people thought it was all part of the play – the shot (if they heard it at all) and Booth's dramatic leap to the stage.

Booth rushed into the alley, grabbed the reigns to his horse from (Peanut) John Burroughs, knocked him to the ground, and headed out at full gallop through the streets of the Capitol.

Major Rathbone picked himself up and unbarred the door to the President's box. Miss Harris shouted, "The President is shot."

By this time several doctors had arrived, and begun to assess the President's condition. They laid him on the floor and began to strip off his clothes. Moments later they discovered a bullet lodged in his skull. The ball entered the back of his head, behind the left ear, and embedded itself in his brain.

When the doctors discovered the source of the wound, they determined to remove Lincoln to the nearest bed and do whatever they could to comfort him. They carried Lincoln out of the theater. A man across the street invited them to use his room, so they took the President in and laid him on a bed. Surgeon Charles Taft, said it was a gruesome scene. As they carried Lincoln, "blood [was] dripping from the wound, faster and faster."

Inside Petersen House, friends and family held a vigil over the dying Lincoln. Surgeon Charles Taft spent most of the night holding the President's head, so blood and brain tissue could continue to ooze out, and prevent clotting. He was relieved several times by surgeon Charles H. Crane.

Lincoln passed away at 7:22 the next morning, April 15th, 1865.

Soldiers wrapped the President's body in a flag taken from the Tenth Street House. His remains were placed in a cart and paraded through the streets of Washington to the White House.

. . . .

Lincoln wasn't the only target that night.

Lewis Thornton Powell rang the bell at William Seward's Mansion about 10:00 PM. He told the doorkeeper he was there to deliver medicine for Seward. Powell made his way upstairs to Seward's bedroom.

Frederick Seward, the son of Secretary Seward, confronted Powell at the top of the stairs. Powell started down the stairs, turned, and attacked Frederick Seward with the butt of his revolver. When he heard the commotion Seward's nurse assistant, Sergeant George E. Robinson, rushed out to help. Powell struck him in the forehead with his knife and raced to Secretary Seward's bed, where he stabbed him three times in the neck.

As Powell was getting ready to strike Seward again, Sergeant Robinson and Major August H. Seward pulled him away. Powell broke free, and made his escape, stabbing a messenger as he ran out of the house.

Alone, and without assistance Powell hid out in a nearby cemetery for three days. Not knowing where to meet up with his fellow conspirators, he returned to the one place he knew they frequented – Mary Surratt's Washington boarding house. His timing couldn't have been worse. When he arrived there, authorities were searching the boarding house. Both Lewis Powell and Mary Surratt were taken into custody.

George A. Atzerodt had a room at Kirkwood House, located just below vice-President Andrew Johnson's. His job was to kill the Vice-President. Instead, he got drunk and wandered the streets of Washington. Soldiers later discovered Atzerodt hiding in the home of a relative.

Michael O'Laughlen boarded General Ulysses S. Grant's train to Philadelphia on the afternoon of April 14th, 1865. His mission was to kill Grant, but he couldn't gain access to Grant's private car because it was locked and guarded by porters.

PURSUIT, CAPTURE, AND DEATH OF JOHN WILKES BOOTH

Washington went into a panic as news of Lincoln's assassination, and the attack on Secretary Seward leaked out.

Secretary of War, Edwin M. Stanton declared martial law.

Union troops guarded every exit into and out of the city. Outgoing trains were stopped and searched. Mounted police and cavalry patrolled the streets. Nearby forts were on high alert, and the siege guns manned awaiting a possible Confederate attack.

A massive manhunt was mounted to search out the conspirators. Secretary of War Edwin Stanton quickly placed a $100,000 reward on the heads of the conspirators.

John Wilkes Booth and David Herold met up at Surratt's Tavern shortly after midnight on the night of the assassination. From there, they rode about twenty miles to the home of Dr. Samuel Mudd. Mudd dressed Booth's wounded leg and crafted a crutch for him. They left at 4:00 PM the next afternoon.

Sunday morning Booth and Herold made the fifteen-mile ride to the home of Captain Samuel Cox, a Southern sympathizer. Booth convinced Cox to help them cross the Potomac. Cox instructed them to hide in the nearby pine thickets. Later, he returned with food and guided them to the home of Thomas A. Jones, who lived at a place called Huckleberry.

Jones cared for Booth and Herold for almost a week while he waited for an opportunity to take them across the Potomac. When he couldn't take them across the river, they made their way to Port Conway. Once there, they joined up with three Confederate soldiers returning home from the war—M. D. Ruggles, Prentiss Ingraham, and Captain William Jett.

The three men agreed to help Booth and Herold cross the river. They secured them a ride on a scow run by Peyton Washington. That night, they slept in the woods outside of Richard Garrett's farm. The next day they visited Garrett and asked for food and shelter.

Ruggles said Booth told him he originally planned to kidnap Lincoln and carry him across Confederate lines. Once there, he assumed they would be able to settle the war on their terms with such a hostage. "Failing this, he decided at the last moment…to strike deadly blows at Mr. Lincoln, Mr. Seward, and General Grant." His intent was not to kill vice president Andrew Johnson but to implicate him in the plot. That was why he visited him the morning of the assassination and left his calling card.

In Washington, Lieutenant Edward P. Doherty, and twenty-four men from the 16th New York Cavalry set off in pursuit of Booth and the other conspirators. He says he went to Port Conway and saw Mrs. Rollins, the ferryman's wife. "Drawing Booth's picture from my pocket I showed it to [her] and inferred from [her] looks that Booth was not very distant."

The ferryman told Lieutenant Doherty he took five men across the river, including Captain William Jett. Doherty located Jett at Goldman's Hotel in Bowling Green. Jett said he left Booth at Garrett's farm. That was at midnight. Even though his men were exhausted after having ridden twenty-four hours without sleep, Doherty had his men saddle up their horses and headed off for Garrett's farm.

They halted at the orchard fence outside of the farm. Doherty sent six soldiers to patrol behind the outbuildings. Their instructions were not to let anyone pass until they gave the countersign, "Corbett." The rest of the troops passed through the gate and surrounded the house.

Doherty dismounted from his horse and knocked on the door. The senior Garrett answered the door. When asked where the fugitives were, he said: "in the fields." The soldiers searched the house and found Garrett's son, who told them the men were in the barn.

The soldiers surrounded the barn. Doherty says he kicked the door but received no answer.

He opened the door and hollered in. Booth refused to come out. Doherty had a corporal gather up some straw and hay, and he set the building on fire.

As the fire increased in intensity, Booth hollered out, "O captain! There is a man in here who wants to surrender awful bad." Herold rushed through the door. Doherty grabbed his wrists and dragged him out of the way.

Doherty heard a shot. His first thought was, "Booth had shot himself."

The straw behind Booth was on fire. Doherty said Booth, "had a crutch, and he held a carbine in his hand. I rushed into the burning barn, followed by my men, and as he was falling caught him under the arms and pulled him out of the barn."

Sergeant Boston Corbett made the fatal shot. He said he watched Booth through a large crack in the barn. He saw Booth level his carbine, and thought he was going to shoot either Herold or Doherty. Corbett fired at

Booth's arm, hoping to disable him. The bullet missed its mark and hit Booth in the back of the head.

Booth was shot at 3:15 AM on April 26th, 1865. He died at 7:00 AM. His last words were, "Tell my mother I died for my country and … I did what I thought was best." Later he muttered – "Useless. Useless." And then he expired.

Lieutenant Doherty reported: "He had on his person a diary, a large Bowie knife, two pistols, a compass, and a draft on a Canadian bank for £60."

Booth's body was sewn up in a horse blanket, and loaded onto a wagon. They took the body to the Washington Navy Yard on the steamer, John S. Ide, and later transferred to the deck of the Ironclad Montauk where doctors performed an autopsy. They interred Booth's remains in a cemetery at the Navy Yard.

The manhunt for Lincoln's assassin was over.

CREATING A NATION OF ADDICTS

Trrue, or false?

Back in the late 1800's and early 1900's you could walk into the corner drug store and buy a do it yourself druggie kit complete with a hypodermic needle, and vials of opium and morphine? The original formula for Coca-Cola™ contained real cocaine? Bayer Pharmaceuticals aggressively marketed heroin beginning in 1899 touting it as a cure for headaches, tuberculosis, menstrual cramps, and more?

True, true, and true again.

Let's try another one.

Drugs weren't a real problem in America until the 1960's. It was that damned Rock 'N Roll music that spawned the Hippie movement, marijuana, LSD, cocaine, and heroin addiction. Before the 1960's Americans didn't do drugs, right?

Wrong again!

Here's the real scoop on addiction in America.

. . . .

Historians can trace the use of marijuana as far back as the writings of Chinese Emperor Shen Nung somewhere around 2700 BC. The Emperor said marijuana was used as a cure for rheumatism, gout, malaria, and even absent-mindedness.

The Spanish conquistadores brought cannabis to America with them in the early 1500's, and records from the Jamestown Colony in 1611 show cannabis was the second largest crop grown there next to tobacco. Hemp was one of George Washington's largest cash crops at his Mount Vernon plantation.

For nearly 150 years patent medicines were used and abused by a large portion of the American public. One of the most popular of these medications was laudanum. Laudanum was a potent mixture of 90% alcohol and 10% opiates. Famous laudanum abusers include Edgar Allan Poe and Mary Todd Lincoln.

Laudanum was sold over-the-counter as a cure for almost any ailment out there—cramps, headaches, aches, pains, you name it. Women were especially susceptible to laudanum addiction as it was a common prescription for female problems, menstrual cramps, and depression.

Morphine was created somewhere around 1810 and was named after the Greek god Morpheus (the god of dreams) because it took people away to a dreamlike state. Morphine soon became the miracle drug of its day and doctors used it to treat severe pain.

In wartime, America morphine was a quick fix for soldiers who had their arms and legs shot off. It offered quick relief from the pain, and was supposed to be "non-addictive." But as doctors soon discovered, that wasn't the case. Morphine users needed larger and more frequent doses to get the same degree of relief.

After the Civil War, morphine became the drug of choice in America. Two to five percent of the adult population was addicted to morphine in the post-war years between 1865 and 1900.

Bayer Pharmaceuticals, a German company, began marketing Heroin in November of 1898. To be fair, they didn't create heroin.

Charles Romley Alder Wright, an English chemist, was the first to synthesize heroin in 1874, but he didn't do anything with his creation.

Bayer recognized the medicine's potential after conducting tests on animals and some of their employees. Not surprisingly, their employees loved heroin. The consensus was it made them feel like superheroes.

By the late 19th century so many doctors had prescribed morphine that America was a nation of morphine addicts. Because morphine addiction was such a huge problem, Bayer felt the biggest market for heroin was as a cure for morphine addiction. It was as easy to buy as aspirin is today. Every corner drug store sold morphine kits.

Bayer touted heroin as a "non-addictive" substitute for morphine. They also promised the drug could cure tuberculosis, cough, colds, cancer, mental illness, old age; you name it. At the turn of the century, you could walk into a store and buy heroin chewing gum, heroin cough drops, heroin cough syrup, and heroin pills. It didn't matter if you were a man, woman, or child, as long as you had the required payment.

The only problem was as early as 1899 studies confirmed heroin was more addictive than morphine. In 1899 Horatio Woods, Jr. noted heroin was addictive. To get the same effect, patients needed stronger doses. Two other early studies noted similar effects about heroin use. One was a 1903 report in the Alabama Journal of Medicine, and the other a 1911 study in the Kentucky Medical Journal.

Surprisingly enough at the height of this controversy, the American Medical Association (AMA) gave its blessings to heroin in 1907.

After continued complaints about heroin addiction, Bayer gave into public pressures and stopped selling heroin in 1913.

....

John Pemberton, a Civil War veteran created Coca-Cola™ created in the 1880's. The original version contained real cocaine and was sold as a patent medicine. Pemberton touted it as a cure for morphine addiction, headaches, impotence, and similar diseases.

Relief from pain and suffering cost just five cents a bottle.

Rumor has it the company removed most of the active cocaine ingredients in 1904, and all traces disappeared by 1929.

．．．．．．．．．．．．．．

The big news today concerns legalizing medicinal and recreational uses of marijuana. What most people forget is for most of America's past marijuana doctors prescribed marijuana as a cure for neuralgia, gonorrhea, headaches, asthma, bronchitis, and menstrual cramps. There's even some talk George Washington used it to relieve the pains he experienced from toothaches.

Recreational use of marijuana wasn't considered a major problem until the early 1900's. Mexican's fleeing the revolution in 1910 ignited the trend here. Because of its ties to illegal immigrants, lots of research was done that tied marijuana use to crime, violence, and other deviant behaviors. By 1930 Twenty-nine states passed laws banning marijuana usage.

In 1936 French director Louis Gasnier released the film *Reefer Madness*. The movie was a cautionary tale about the effects of marijuana use on high school students. One student gets high and runs a pedestrian over. Later he is told the person died and felt no remorse. Other scenes depict students driven to rape, suicide, and madness because of marijuana use. In the final scene, the school principle warns another student not to let these things happen to them.

The next year Congress passed the Marijuana Tax Act which effectively criminalized marijuana use. The Boggs Act in 1952 and the Narcotics Control Act of 1960 made a first offense for marijuana use punishable by a mandatory sentence of two to ten years in prison and a fine of up to $20,000.

In 1970 Congress repealed the minimum sentences imposed for marijuana use, and in the following decades, many states decriminalized marijuana usage completely.

. . . .

So, the next time you're watching the evening news with grandma, and she tells you how much better it was in the old days because they didn't have all these temptations—tell her, "not so."

AMERICAN CHARACTERS

From the country's very beginning, Americans had proven to be a unique breed. They were optimistic and forward-thinking. Even the poor and homeless, who lived on the streets, or in dirt shelters on the frontier, were obsessed with the idea they could better themselves. Overall, Americans were hopeful. They believed that with a lot of effort, and hard work, and maybe just a touch of luck, they could better their situation in life. At the very least, every generation could rest assured, knowing their children would live a better life than they had.

Visitors to the country wrote about America's obsession with business and money. They described Americans as hurried and rushed for time, violent and immoral. To the rest of the world, Americans appeared to be money grubbers who didn't give a damn about social conventions. And, nowhere was this obsession more noticeable than on the western frontier.

Life was cheap on the frontier.

Men carried weapons everywhere they went. They followed the scent of silver and gold, moving from mining camp to mining camp. If someone got in your way, you shot first and asked questions later. That was the code of the west.

Some characters were good, some not so good. Others straddled the line between good and evil.

Johnny Appleseed embraced all that was good in the American character. He moved on the edge of the frontier, planting orchards two to three years in advance of the settler's arrival. That way Johnny had new seedlings available when they were needed. He was welcomed into pioneer homes and spread his brand of religion wherever he went. Several times he warned villages about impending Indian attacks that saved dozens of lives.

Wild Bill Hickok was a frontier lawman whose skill with a gun helped him clean up Hays City and Dodge City, Kansas. The story is one hundred men met their end at the barrel of his pistols. His life encompassed the entire frontier experience rolled up into the life of one man. He served as an army scout and spy in the Civil War, Indian fighter, frontier lawman, gunfighter, gambler, and drunk. Towards the end of his life when his vision failed him, Bill acted in Buffalo Bill's Wild West Show, made his way west to Deadwood in the Dakota, Territory, to try his hand at mining. He died playing poker at Nuttal and Mann's Saloon.

Bat Masterson was a frontier lawman who played both sides of the law. During the early days, when he was sheriff of Dodge City, Masterson cleaned up the town and rooted out the rift-raft. He traded his pistols for a pen and covered sporting events for several major newspapers. Later, Masterson became a sports promoter—and sponsored many of the big-name boxers of his day. But, trouble seemed to follow Masterson. He was accused repeatedly of rigging boxing matches, and other games of chance. Despite all his nefarious dealings, most people today consider Bat Masterson one of the good guys.

Go figure?

Calamity Jane was a frontier Hellcat—more male than female, who rode with Custer's scouts, fought Indians, carried the mail, gambled, and drank like a man. She was the subject of Frontier Dime Novels, and her daring deeds were well-known throughout the east and west. Here's the thing—her exploits may have been more fiction than fact.

General George Armstrong Custer had it all. By the end of the Civil War, he was the best-known general in the army other than Ulysses S. Grant. Custer played a major role in the Confederate surrender at Appomattox Court House, rode on to fame—leading the 7th Cavalry in the Plains Indian Wars, and was rumored to be a presidential contender for the 1876 election. His death on the Little Big Horn is still a hotly debated topic 140 years later.

And, last, but not least, we come to Charles Julius Guiteau, the assassin of President James Garfield. Guiteau was a failed lawyer, a drifter from Illinois who made his way to Washington seeking a government office. When that didn't happen, he said he received a vision that the country would be better off if he "removed" Garfield. At his trial Guiteau raced about like a madman—he accused the president's doctors of malpractice and of killing Garfield. On the witness stand, prosecutors questioned Guiteau about how God inspired his actions. The press ate it up. It was the first celebrity trial on record.

JOHNNY APPLESEED – MAN, MYTH, AND LEGEND

Much like Daniel Boone, Davy Crockett, and other frontier legends,

Johnny Appleseed is one of those mythical characters every school child learns about. His story has become so entwined in the folklore surrounding him; it is difficult to unravel truth from fiction.

What we do know is he was born John Chapman, in Leonidas, Massachusetts, on September 26, 1774. His father was a Minuteman in the Revolutionary War. He fought at Bunker Hill, as well as serving with Washington's troops in New York. His mother died in 1776, most likely from tuberculosis.

Sometime in 1797, or 1798, Johnny made his way to western Pennsylvania where he planted his first orchard on Brokenstraw Creek. A few years later, he was living near French Creek and planted several orchards near there.

Johnny Appleseed was a shrewd businessman. He seeded orchards several steps in advance of settlers moving into new territories, so he could have young apple trees ready for the settlers when they arrived.

An article published in *Harper's New Monthly Magazine* in 1871 said: "Johnny would shoulder his bag of apple seeds, and with bare feet penetrate to some remote spot that combined the picturesque and fertility of soil, and there he would plant his seeds, place a slight inclosure around the place, and leave them to grow until the trees were large enough to be transplanted by the settlers."

It was the method he would employ for the rest of his life. Johnny studied settlement trends, anticipating where new territories would open—always speculating where the settlers would be two or three years out into the future. Then he would gather up his leather bags full of apple seeds, load them on horseback, or toss them across his shoulders, and trudge off to some remote wilderness area to plant his new orchard. After Johnny planted his seeds, he enclosed them with a fence of logs, fallen timbers, or brush. He would return at regular intervals to mend the fences, check up on his trees, and when the time was right—sell his trees for an average price of five or six cents each.

What surprised people the most was after Johnny did all this work, he sold his trees when possible, but many times he gave them away to people who couldn't afford them, or traded them for food and cast off clothing. Money wasn't his primary objective. Johnny was all about getting his trees into the hands of people who needed them.

Johnny Appleseed didn't give a damn about his looks. If the truth is told—he looked like a crazed lunatic or the perennial "Wildman of the Wilderness." Johnny "had long dark hair, a scraggly beard that was never shaved, and keen black eyes that sparkled with a peculiar brightness." He went everywhere barefoot, even in the harshest winters, though sometimes he was seen walking with a boot on one foot, and a shoe upon the other. In later years "his principal garment was a coffee sack, in which he cut holes for his arms to pass through." And, on his head, he wore a tin pan as a hat.

Strange as it may seem, his odd looks didn't scare people away. By all accounts, the settlers welcomed Johnny into their cabins. Numerous frontier diaries exist that describe a visit from Johnny. He was popular with children and adults alike. Young girls looked forward to his visits, often noting he brought them bright calico cloths and ribbons. He enthralled the men and boys with the stories of his adventures. Many listeners remembered watching Johnny Appleseed perform crazy feats, where he stuck pins and needles into the hardened and leathery skin of his feet.

At night, he would spread himself out on the floor of their cabins and read from books that detailed his religion. One woman, who heard Johnny talk said, "he was undoubtedly a genius."

The Indians considered him a great medicine man and allowed him to travel freely within their lands. Because of this, he saved several settlements from Indian attacks during the War of 1812. One time, he raced thirty miles through the wilderness stopping at every cabin between Mansfield and Mount Vernon, Ohio, to warn people of an impending Indian attack. Undoubtedly, he saved many lives with the early warnings he was able to give.

Johnny was also a man of deep religious convictions. He devoured the religious works of Emanuel Swedenborg; a Swedish scientist turned religious visionary, who believed the final judgment of the world had occurred in 1757. After his spiritual awakening, Swedenborg claimed he could visit heaven and hell whenever he wanted and converse with angels and demons. The central principle of his religion was to do good without seeking a reward for doing so.

Like Swedenborg, Johnny claimed he had frequent conversations with angels and spirits. According to one source, two spirits "of the feminine gender…had revealed to him that they were to be his wives in a future state…" if he avoided marrying in this lifetime.

He was a friend to animals and would buy lame horses, paying someone to feed and care for them, until he could transport them to a safe area, or place them with a helpful owner. He believed every creature had feelings and refused to cut down trees or kill insects.

In March of 1845, Johnny visited the home of William Worth. He curled up to sleep on the cabin floor that night, and never woke up. After his death, his legend continued to grow, until soon—it became difficult to distinguish fact from fiction.

What we do know is at the time of his death, Johnny Appleseed, a man who cared little for money, had accumulated a small fortune in real estate. It is estimated he held over 1200 acres in prime orchard lands in Western Pennsylvania, Ohio, and Indiana.

WILD BILL – JAMES BUTLER HICKOK

Journalist Henry M. Stanley interviewed Wild Bill for a series of articles published in the *St. Louis Democrat* in April of 1867. He wrote, Wild Bill "stands six foot one inch in his moccasins, and is as handsome a specimen of man as could be found." He "held himself straight, and had broad compact, shoulders, was large chested, with small waist, and well-formed muscular limbs."

Stanley asked, "I say, Mr. Hickok, how many men have you killed to your certain knowledge?"

"After a little deliberation, he replied, 'I suppose I have killed considerable over a hundred.'"

"What made you kill all those men? Did you kill them without cause or provocation?"

"No, by heaven I have never killed one man without good cause."

Later in the interview, Wild Bill described his first kill to Stanley.

He was lying in bed in a hotel room in Leavenworth, Kansas when he heard a commotion outside of his door. Bill grabbed his six-shooter and a Bowie knife and remained under his covers. "The door was opened, and five men entered the room. I kept perfectly still until just as the knife touched my breast; I sprang aside and buried mine in his heart, and used

138

my revolver on the others right and left." When the shooting stopped, Bill ran out of the room and kept running until he reached Fort Leavenworth.

James Butler Hickok earned the moniker "Wild Bill" in an 1862 showdown with Davis McCandles, his brother William, and several of their hired hands. The story is the boys caught up with Wild Bill at the stage station and demanded he pay a debt he owed them. The talk soon turned to gunplay. When it was over, the two McCandles brothers and one of their accomplices lay dead in the street.

The *Atchison Daily Champion* from February 5th, 1862 wrote, "Wild Bill…shot McKandles through the heart with a rifle, and then stepping out of doors, revolver in hand shot another one of the gang dead; severely wounded a third…and slightly wounded the fourth."

When the shooting stopped, and Bill finished nursing his wounds, he told friends, "I just got wild and slashed about like a bear with a death wound." The next thing you know, James Butler Hickok became better known as Wild Bill.

After the McCandles fight, Bill made his way to Leavenworth, Kansas, where he became a Brigade Wagon Master for General John Charles Fremont, trucking supplies out of Fort Leavenworth. Sometime in 1863 he became a Union spy and helped to gather information from behind the Confederate lines.

At the end of the Civil War, Wild Bill drifted into Missouri and faced down Davis Tutt in the Town Square of Springfield, Missouri on July 21st, 1865. It was one of the classic gunfights pictured in every western film since the beginning of time. The two men stood fifteen paces apart, staring each other down in the hot sun. They reached for their guns. One man lay dead in the street. The other walked away.

Here's how it started.

Wild Bill and Tutt sat across from each other, engaged in a high-stakes card game. When Bill won a big hand, Tutt reminded him about some money he owed him. Bill paid up. A few moments later, Tutt brought up another debt Hickok owed him. Tutt grabbed Wild Bill's gold pocket watch and said he'd hold on to it until Bill settled the debt.

Wild Bill challenged Tutt to a duel in the town square. An account, published in the February 1867 issue of *Harper's New Monthly Magazine*, said "Tutt then showed his pistol. Bill kept a sharp eye on him, and before Tutt could Pint it Bill had his'n out.

"At that moment, you could have heard a pin drop in that squar. Both Tutt and Bill fired, but one discharge followed the other so quick that it's hard to say which went off first. Tutt was a famous shot, but he missed this time; the ball from the pistol went over Bill's head. The instant Bill fired, without waiting ter see of he had hit Tutt, he wheeled on his heels and pointed his pistol at Tutt's friends, who had already drawn their weapons."

Wild Bill earned his reputation as a fast gun that day.

Bill entered a country saloon in Jefferson County, Missouri in 1867. Five cowboys picked a fight with him. One of the boys snuck up behind Bill, gave him a shove that made him spill his beer, and almost sent him tumbling to the ground. Bill wheeled around, bloodied the cowboy's nose, and sent him crashing to the floor.

Bill challenged the four remaining cowboys to a duel outside. He shot one of them right off but took a ball in his arm. In an instant, he shifted his gun to the other hand, then dropped the other three. Four men lay dead in the street. Another was severely wounded.

On September 8th, 1869, Bill was elected city marshal of Hays City, Kansas, one of the toughest towns on the frontier. Not long after that, Sam

Strangham approached Wild Bill at a local saloon and pulled his Navy Colt. Bill got off the first shot, and fired his derringer into Strangham's left eye. "The man was stone dead on his feet, falling forward onto his face without even a twitch of the muscles."

Later, in December, a bully named Bill Mulvey went on a wild, drunken bender, terrorizing the town—breaking windows with a club, threatening the townspeople, and reportedly chasing two constables to the city limits. Mulvey got the drop on Wild Bill. He held two pistols to his head. Bill faked him out. He whispered to an imaginary constable behind Mulvey, telling him to kill him. When Mulvey turned to look, Wild Bill blew his brains out.

On February 12th, 1870, Wild Bill got into a tussle with some soldiers from the Seventh Cavalry at Paddy Welch's Saloon. He killed several of the soldiers and wounded a few more. During the fight, Bill took a total of seven balls in his arms and legs. After his recovery, Wild Bill hid out for a while, because General Sheridan had put out an order for him to be brought in "dead or alive." When the Seventh Cavalry pulled out of Fort Hays several months later, Bill returned to Kansas and was appointed marshal of Abilene.

On October 7th, 1871, the *Junction City Union* reported a gunfight in the Alamo, "a gambling hell." City Marshal Wild Bill "fired with marvelous rapidity and characteristic accuracy." Several men were shot and killed including, Phil Cole, and Jack Harvey. A policeman, Jim McWilliams, rushed in to help. Bill accidentally shot, and killed him.

After he killed McWilliams, Bill hung up his guns and tried his hand at acting. In the fall of 1872, he joined Buffalo Bill and Texas Jack, in a series of western reenactments staged by dime novelist Ned Buntline. In 1873 – 1874 he joined with Buffalo Bill to perform in his "Scouts of the

Plains." But, Buffalo Bill said Wild Bill wasn't much of an actor. Every time he "went upon the stage before an audience, it was almost impossible for him to utter a word."

Bill drifted for a while. In 1876 he tried his luck at mining in the Black Hills. Eventually, Bill wound up in Deadwood, Dakota Territory, where he spent much of his time gambling in Nuttal & Mann's Saloon. Sometime around 3:00 PM on August 2nd, 1876, Bill was playing poker with his back to the door, something he rarely did. Jack McCall sidled up behind Wild Bill. Before anyone could see what he did, McCall pulled out a large pistol. "The ball went crashing through the back of Bill's head and came out at the center of his right cheek…Wild Bill dropped his head forward; the cards fell from his relaxing grip, and, in a succession of slow movements, he slipped out of the chair and fell prone upon the floor."

The man who claimed to have killed over one hundred men lay dead on the floor. His final hand, a pair of aces and eights, became known as the "dead man's hand."

"BAT" MASTERSON – THIS WESTERN LAWMAN OUTLIVED THEM ALL

Today we think of Bat Masterson as a frontier good guy, but in his day, the press wasn't so sure which side of the law Bat was on. The *Globe Republican* (Dodge City) wrote, "Bat is one of the best-known sports in the West and has had a checkered career ever since he came into prominence as a city marshal of Dodge City when it was a cowboy town."

Years later, in 1905, when Masterson became a deputy marshal in New York on the recommendation of Teddy Roosevelt, the *Washington Times* suggested his selection was a bit of ridiculous overkill. They said, "The action is somewhat similar to that of Congress when it passed a $50,000,0000 appropriation bill for national defenses and called it a 'peace measure,' shortly after the blowing up of the Battleship Maine."

Or, maybe it was an extension of Theodore Roosevelt's trademark phrase, "speak softly, and carry a big stick." Only the *Times* understood *you couldn't fight criminals by inviting a killer to the party.* Appointing Bat Masterson as a deputy marshal was a lot like throwing down a challenge to the criminal class, especially if you factored in Bat's troubled past.

William Barclay Masterson made his way to the Kansas Frontier in 1871 at the tender young age of eighteen. He worked as a buffalo hunter, a civilian scout for General Nelson A. Miles in his Indian campaigns, and not too many years after that as a frontier lawman.

In 1874, Bat took part in the Second Battle of Adobe Walls—an epic standoff between 27 buffalo hunters and 700 Comanche, Cheyenne, Kiowa, and Arapaho warriors.

Adobe Walls was an obscure trading post located in the middle of the Texas Panhandle. At the time of the fight, it consisted of three haphazard buildings—Frederick Leonard's store, James Hanrahan's saloon, and Tom O'Keefe's blacksmith shop.

In late spring of 1874, buffalo hunters invaded the Llano Estacado and killed over 100,000 buffalo in a short period. The Indians, led by Quanah Parker, pushed back over the loss of their food supply. They first attacked a small hunter's camp, then moved on to Adobe Walls.

The warriors split off into four separate bands. One group struck O'Keefe's blacksmith shop, which had four men, and a woman, hidden inside.

Ten people barricaded themselves inside Hanrahan's building, seven of them armed with Buffalo fifty caliber guns. James Hanrahan passed the order not to fire until the Indians came within 30 yards.

Another band rushed Frederick Leonard's building where the door stood wide open when the attack started. At the first shot, Leonard ran into his store. Sam Smith made it inside just as the doors were being slammed shut. Close behind him were Quanah Parker and 25 warriors who slammed their bodies against the door but couldn't break it down.

Just north of the stockade, Ike and Shorty Shadler slept in their wagon, unaware the Indians had laid siege to Adobe Walls. The Indians snuck up on the two men, killed and scalped them as they slept, then scalped the brother's dog for good measure.

Back at Adobe Walls, 25 warriors rode up to O'Keefe's, dismounted, and rushed the building. The men inside opened fire. Across the way, Billy Dixon and Bat Masterson poured a deadly fire into the attackers from their position at Hanrahan's store.

Despite their mounting losses, the Indians continued to charge the building in small groups of two to five for most of the day.

On day two of the siege, the defenders abandoned Hanrahan's place and split up among the other buildings. Later that night, a hunter named Reed volunteered for a suicide mission. He raced out of the building after dark and made a mad dash towards Dodge City to summon help.

Beginning at sunrise on the third day, the Indians launched a series of small attacks. William Olds was killed during one of the charges. He fell through a trap door on the roof and landed dead at the feet of his wife inside.

By 5 AM on the fourth day of the siege, 100 buffalo hunters arrived to reinforce Adobe Walls.

On the morning of July 14th, the Indian warriors lifted the siege and rode away. The hunters didn't waste any time getting out of there. They set out on foot for Dodge City. Eighty Indians, four white men, and 200 Indian ponies lay dead on the battlefield.

Years later, the *Salt Lake Herald* shared this story about Bat Masterson at Adobe Walls. A man named Shepherd tried to shoot an Indian "six times, and missed him every time." Having no success, he asked Bat to give it a whirl.

"I saw Mr. Indian breaking my way," said Bat, "getting out of range of fire from Bob Wright's store. I commenced getting a bead on him. As he backed an inch or two more I let fly, and Mr. Indian bounded in the air about 3 feet, dropped his rifle and fell dead."

And, with that shot, Bat Masterson stepped on the stage into frontier history.

Masterson's first recorded kill occurred at the Lady Gay saloon in Sweetwater, Texas, on the evening of January 24th, 1876. He was playing a game of poker with Harry Fleming, Jim Duffy, and Corporal Melvin King. King soon left, apparently frustrated, because he was losing.

Bat, Charlie Norton, and a working girl named Mollie Brennan walked across the street to Charlie Norton's dance hall. Someone pounded on the door. Bat went to answer it. Melvin King pushed his way in—revolver in hand, cursing at Bat. Mollie quickly jumped between the two men just as King pulled the trigger. His first bullet missed Mollie and hit Masterson smack dab in the belly. King's second shot sent Mollie tumbling to the floor—dead. That bought Bat the time he needed to pull his pistol. Melvin King hit the floor—fatally wounded.

The shooting was quickly ruled self-defense. Bat never had much to say about it. In 1881, he told the *Kansas City Journal*, "I had a little difficulty with some soldiers down there, but never mind; I dislike to talk about it."

By early June of 1877, Bat found himself in another scrape, this time in Dodge City. "Robert Gilmore was making a talk for himself in a rather emphatic manner, to which Marshal Deger took exceptions, and started for the dog house [jail] with him. Bobby walked very leisurely—so much so that Larry felt it necessary to administer a few personal kicks. This was soon interrupted by Bat Masterson, who wound his arm affectionately

146

around the marshal's neck and let the prisoner escape." Deger then got in a row with Bat.

Joe Mason grabbed Bat's gun. Bat did his damnedest to get another one from the crowd. Seeing that the marshal was in trouble, several cowboys came to his aid and held Bat down. That "gave him [marshal Deger] a chance to draw his gun and beat Bat over the head until blood flew" all over.

The *Dodge City Times* reported, "Bat Masterson seemed possessed of extraordinary strength, every inch of the way was closely contested, but the city dungeon was reached at last, and in he went. If he had got hold of his gun before going in, there would have been a general killing."

Ironically, the same issue of the *Dodge City Times* that featured Bat's arrest announced his brother Ed's appointment as assistant marshal of Dodge City. The paper said, "He is not very large, but there are not many men who would be anxious to tackle him a second time. He makes a good officer."

In early November of 1877, Bob Shaw got it into his head to take Texas Dick down a few bars at the Lone Star Saloon. When Ed Masterson entered the saloon, he discovered Bob Shaw with "a huge pistol in one hand and a hogshead of blood in his right eye, ready to relieve Texas Dick of his existence in this world."

Ed tried to find a peaceful solution. "Officer Masterson then gently tapped the belligerent Shaw upon the back of the head with the butt of his shooting iron, merely to convince him of the vanities of this frail world and to teach him that all isn't lovely." The smack on the head "didn't have the desired effect, and instead of dropping, as any man of fine sensibilities would have done, Shaw turned his battery [gun] upon the officer and let him have it in the right breast." The shot knocked Ed's right arm out of commission, but as he fell, he got off a few well place shots with his left hand, hitting Shaw in the "left hand and left leg."

Texas Dick took a bullet to the groin, "making a painful and dangerous, though not necessarily a fatal wound." A bystander by the name of Frank Buskirk got a little too close to the action and wound up taking a bullet to his left arm.

In the end, the *Dodge City Times* reported, "Nobody was killed, but for a time it looked as though the undertaker and the coroner would have something to do." They commended Deputy Marshal Masterson for his bravery.

Later that same month, on November 24th, 1877, Bat Masterson was elected sheriff of Ford County, Kansas. The *Dodge City Times* described the new sheriff as "cool, decisive, and a bad man with a pistol."

The *New York Times* later commented, "It took a man with a reputation to be sheriff of Ford County." If that was the case, Bat Masterson was a perfect choice.

In those days, Dodge City was still a rough and tumble cattle town. Cowboys ruled Dodge City from July to November when they drove the big herds into town fresh off the Chisolm Trail. By the time, they reached Dodge City, the cowboys needed to blow off some steam. Many of them rode into the city—firing six-shooters and rifles into the air. After they had disposed of their horses, most of the cowboys walked off in search of drinks, smokes, and some close companionship from a dancehall girl.

Shortly after 10 PM on the night of April 9th, 1878, shots rang out from the south side of the tracks. Deputy Marshal Ed Masterson and policeman Haywood rushed to the scene and found six cowboys newly arrived in town. Masterson discovered one of the cowboys, by the name of Jack Wagner, was carrying a six-shooter contrary to city ordinance. He disarmed the man and turned the weapon over to the cattle boss, A. M. Walker.

Later that same evening, Masterson met Wagner outside of a dance hall and noticed he was once again carrying a pistol. He attempted to take it from him. Policeman Haywood rushed forward to assist, but as he did, several cowboys shoved a gun in his face and held him back. Someone fired a shot into his face, but luckily for officer Haywood, it misfired.

Seconds later, Wagner fired a round into Ed Masterson's abdomen. Five shots followed in quick succession.

Jack Wagner staggered into Peacock's saloon—gut shot. He would soon die from the wound. A. W. Walker, Wagner's trail boss, took a bullet in his left lung, and several more in his right arm. He escaped into Peacock's saloon and was left for dead.

Ed Masterson made his way across the street to Hoover's Saloon, staggered up to George Hinkle, and told him, "George, I'm shot!" The *Leavenworth Weekly Times* reported, "His clothes were still on fire from the discharge of the pistol, which had been placed against the right side of his abdomen and 'turned loose,' making a hole large enough for the introduction of the whole pistol. The ball passed completely through him, leaving him no possible chance for life."

The big question is: Who shot Jack Wagner and A. M. Walker? Legend tells us it was Bat Masterson. *Years later, the Arizona Republican* wrote, Bat killed the seven men responsible for his brother's death in as many minutes. The murderers locked the doors to the saloon when they saw him coming. "Masterson jumped square against the door with both feet bursting it open at the first attempt. Then sprang inside firing immediately right and left. Four dropped dead in a shorter time than it requires to tell it." The other three outlaws ran for their horses trying desperately to escape. "Before they reached the outskirts of the town all three had bitten the dust."

It's a great story!

But, guess what? It never happened. I read every newspaper account published in 1878 that mentioned the Masterson's, and Bat's name didn't come up one time as having avenged Ed. Not once!

Instead, newspaper accounts left things rather vague. All three participants stagger away into nearby saloons to take their final curtain call. All we know for certain is six gunshots rang out in quick succession. Jack Wagner nailed Ed Masterson. But, who shot Wagner and Walker is left to our imaginations. All the stories implied Ed Masterson took down his killers before he died. But, that's as far as it goes. What really happened is anyone's guess.

In mid-April of 1881, Bat got in a tangle with A. J. Peacock and Al Updegraff on the main streets in Dodge City. The *Las Vegas Morning Gazette* wrote, "the cause was a private quarrel." Bat's brother Jim was a partner in the Lady Gay Dance Hall and Saloon with A. J. Peacock. Peacock hired his brother-in-law, Al Updegraff, as a bartender, against the wishes of Jim Masterson. In no time the matter escalated, and Bat found himself rushing back to Dodge City to protect brother Jim.

The way it all played out, Bat arrived in town by train on April 16, 1881. Suspecting there might be some foul play, he slipped out of the train just before it pulled into the depot. As he rounded the corner, Bat encountered Updegraff and Peacock. Gunfire soon broke out, and for several minutes downtown, Dodge City sounded like a war zone.

Mayor Webster and Marshal Singer eventually arrested Bat. He was fined $8.00, and another $2.00 for court costs, and allowed to leave town, along with his brother Jim.

It was evident Bat had worn out his welcome. The *Dodge City Times* made it clear Bat Masterson was persona non-grata. "The firing on the street by Bat Masterson, and jeopardizing the lives of citizens, is severely condemned by our people, and the good opinion many citizens had of Bat has been changed to one of contempt."

In the fall of 1883, New York Police Superintendent Thomas Byrnes summoned Bat to the city. One of the city's prominent millionaires, George Gould, was being shadowed by a suspicious character, and the city's detectives weren't having any luck catching him. Superintendent Byrnes said he chose Bat because he "would not be afraid to shoot a man on a crowded Broadway and who would be certain to hit the right man."

Bat pursued his man for eight months before finally bringing the man to justice. The man arrested at the home of Helen Gould said she had promised to marry him. Apparently, he was a "lunatic." But, a smart one, if he could evade the entire New York City police force and Bat Masterson for nearly a year.

Much more could be written about Bat Masterson and his law enforcement work, but just like a cat, Bat lived nine lives—continually reinventing himself.

In 1883, Bat Masterson gave up the gun, for a much stronger weapon— the pen. The *Dodge City Times* said, "The fine artistic style in which Col. Bat wields the pen is adding fame to his already illustrious name."

And, though he would continue writing for the rest of his life, Bat soon added another notch on his resume—sports promoter.

Boxing, especially, became one of Bat's great passions. In 1888, while refereeing a bout between John P. Clow and Jim Fell, Bat called a questionable foul. Even so, "the crowd received the announcement with shouts of approval," wrote the *Omaha Daily Bee*, "as it was a well-known fact that anyone who questioned any of Masterson's acts never survived a great length of time to talk about it."

In 1893, the *Globe-Republican* speculated it was Masterson who won the Goddard-Smith boxing match in New Orleans. Bat said "he knew Smith had a yellow streak in him" so he stayed in Smith's corner all night. Some reporters suggested Bat pulled his gun in the ring and told the boxer "If you quit, I'll blow your head off." In which case, it was a smoking gun that won the contest, not the pugilist.

Charges of crooked sporting contests would follow Bat for the rest of his life. In 1902, Masterson got arrested for possessing crooked gambling instruments. Also, arrested were his partners in crime, James A. Sullivan, J. F. Saunders, and Leopold Frank. Their accuser was a Chicago man by the name of Snow who said they swindled him out of $17,000 in a game at the Waldorf.

Bat eventually beat the rap and got off with a $10 penalty for possession of a firearm.

In 1903, the Butte Inter Mountain reported Bat won $30,000 at a faro table in Hot Springs, Arkansas. The paper said, "Masterson is a lucky dog and always was. He could win when nobody else could, and he generally picked the winner in the big prize fights."

In 1904, Bat Masterson visited Teddy Roosevelt at the White House. The two men got along splendidly. Bat visited the President every day for a week. They talked about old times in the west, ranching, and sporting events—all subjects dear to Roosevelt.

The next year, when the opportunity arose, Roosevelt repaid Bat by pressuring New York Marshal Hinkel to appoint Bat as Deputy Marshal, a position he held for the next seven years. In his time as a New York marshal, Bat dealt mainly with counterfeiters, moonshiners, and confidence men. One thing he noted was the New York city streets were much more dangerous than any he had ever patrolled in the old west. In New York, every man carried a gun and was dumb enough to use it. In the old west, when a man didn't want to fight, he went around unarmed. That way no one would mess with him. New Yorkers didn't care about honor or fairness. They were quick to shoot, and to kill.

After he left the marshal's office in 1912, Bat returned to his writing. He covered sporting events, politics, local affairs, and sometimes when the spirit moved him he shared memories of daring times in the old west.

The *Butler Weekly Times* best summarized Bat's troubled life. "His skills with the revolver made him invaluable, and no one ever inquired how many toughs tumbled before his never missing muzzle." For a short time, it required men with nerve and pluck to tame the west. As soon as civilization arrived, their usefulness was at an end.

Bat Masterson died at his writing desk on October 25th, 1921. He was 66 years old.

GENERAL GEORGE ARMSTRONG CUSTER ON THE LITTLE BIG HORN

Mention the name George Armstrong Custer and tempers are bound to flare. Many historians have made Custer out to be a martyr. Others have portrayed him as a monster, who sacrificed his troops in the Civil War, to satisfy his quest for everlasting glory.

The truth is probably somewhere in between.

Custer ranked dead last in his class at West Point. But, his timing for attending that institution couldn't have been better. He graduated in 1861 at the start of the Civil War when the Union Army was desperate for new officers. Nearly 35 percent of his class resigned their commissions to return home and fight for the Confederacy.

Custer began the war as an aide to General McClellan. Not long after that, he received a commission as a cavalry officer and received a series of quick promotions due to his boldness in battle. After the Battle of Bull Run, the *New York Tribune* reported Custer had "most of the qualities which go to make up a first-class hero."

What the newspapers didn't mention was Custer loved war. He was invigorated by the sights, sounds, and the smell of battle. While most officers kept to the rear of their troops, Custer led every charge of the Third Michigan—saber in one hand, pistol in the other.

He was reckless with the lives of his men. He didn't plan; he didn't scout out enemy positions. When others urged caution, Custer jumped in. During the Peninsula Campaign when McClellan stopped his troops to determine how deep the waters of the Chickahominy River were, Custer plunged in and rode out to the center. After proving its depth, he rode back to his place in line.

Rather than choose a strategy that would result in the fewest casualties, Custer threw his men at enemy positions, unconcerned about the costs in human life. In his book, *Crazy Horse and Custer*, Stephen Ambrose compared it to a *Cult of Blood*, where Union officers measured their success by how many casualties their troops suffered. He says after General Grant had begun the Wilderness Campaign, the idea was to kill as many Confederates as possible. To hell with the number of Union soldiers killed doing it.

Custer was just the man for the job. When he was unsure what to do— he charged. That's why Abraham Lincoln loved Ulysses S. Grant. While other generals stopped to plan, and determine what they should do next, Grant moved from battle to battle. He didn't let fear of what was over the next hill, or across the next river stop him. He kept moving forward, searching out his next battle.

At Gettysburg, Custer led a charge against a position of Confederate cannon. When his horse was shot from under him, he grabbed another horse and kept fighting. Later in the battle, he had a second horse shot from under him. The fighting soon became hand to hand—with sabers and pistols drawn. Custer's brigade suffered 219 casualties. That night J. E. B. Stuart withdrew his forces and rejoined Lee's army west of Gettysburg.

Towards the end of the war, Custer defeated Jubal Early's army at Waynesboro. A few weeks later he cut off Robert E. Lee's escape route at

Appomattox. His men were first to receive a flag of truce from Lee's forces. For his part in that battle, General Philip Sheridan gave him the table used by Robert E. Lee and General Ulysses S. Grant to sign the terms of surrender.

At the end of the war, Custer returned to the rank of Captain. He served in Texas for a short time, before being stationed with the Seventh Cavalry at Fort Riley, Kansas.

That's where the Custer legend began.

Custer led a winter campaign in 1868. On November 27th, he led an attack against a large village of Cheyenne. The night before the battle his men surrounded the village. The next morning, he had the regimental band strike up "Garry Owen" as the Seventh Cavalry charged into the village. The sleepy Cheyenne were taken by surprise. In less than three hours, over one hundred men, women, and children were killed, including Chief Black Kettle.

The Battle at Washita River was hailed as a victory because it helped to persuade many Cheyenne to move to the reservation. The dark side was Black Kettle, and his followers were friendly Indians under the protection of the commander at Fort Cobb. Although no one said anything about it at the time, the village was located on the Cheyenne reservation—a supposedly safe spot for Black Kettle's band.

In 1868, the Treaty of Laramie promised the Black Hills to the Sioux Nation in perpetuity. The problem was Secretary of Interior, Columbus Delano, believed the Black Hills to be a source of minerals and other untold riches—riches the United States desperately needed to rebuild their struggling economy after the Panic of 1873. When General Alfred Terry ordered the exploration of the Black Hills in June of 1874, Custer was his first choice to command the expedition.

The exploration party consisted of over one thousand troops, one hundred and ten wagons, a photographer, newspaper correspondents, engineers, and several miners. One of the miners, Horatio Ross, discovered gold along French Creek during the last week of July. Custer immediately dispatched word of the find to Fort Laramie. In no time, word of the gold strike spread around the country and the world. A new gold rush was on—smack dab into the Pahá Sápa—the most sacred land of the Sioux.

One outgrowth of the Black Hills gold rush was many Sioux, and Cheyenne left the reservations in a defiant protest of their sacred land being flooded with white miners. They gathered in Montana, under the leadership of Sitting Bull. The Army sent a large force under the command of General Alfred Terry to drive the Indians back onto the reservations.

Terry split his army into a three-pronged column. Custer and the Seventh Cavalry made first contact with the Indians. Early on the morning of June 25th, 1876, Custer's scouts spotted signs of a large Indian encampment in the valley of the Little Bighorn. His scouts advised him the force was too large to attack, but Custer brushed off their warnings. He was determined to make the first strike.

Later that day, Custer split his force of six hundred and forty-seven men into three divisions. He sent Captain Frederick Benteen to scout along a ridge to the left of the Indian encampment. Major Marcus Reno was directed to move up the valley of the Little Bighorn, where he would attack the village. Custer followed the high ground to the right of the valley.

His plan was to encircle the Indians and take them by surprise. Unknown to Custer, the Indians had been tracking his advance for days, waiting for him to make his move.

Reno's command was the first to come under attack. His squadron of one hundred and seventy-five men came under heavy attack at the south end of the village. They quickly withdrew into the timber and brush along the river and continued uphill as that position turned indefensible. What saved them from total annihilation was the arrival of Custer's command. If Custer hadn't happened along, there would have been a second massacre of all Reno's men.

As Custer's men attacked the other side of the encampment, the Indians rushed to meet the new challenge to the north. The main force of Cheyenne and Sioux made a ferocious attack upon his men. As Custer retreated uphill trying to dig his troops in, Crazy Horse and his warriors circled to higher ground to cut them off.

After less than an hour of fierce fighting, all two hundred and ten men in Custer's command lay dead. The *Bismarck Weekly Tribune* described the grisly scene in their July 12th issue. Lieutenant Bradley reported to General Terry, "He had found Custer with one hundred and ninety cavalry men. They lay as they fell, shot down from every side. General Custer shot through the head and body, seemed to have been among the last to fall." All of the non-commissioned men were, "terribly mutilated…The heads of some were severed from the body, the privates of some were cut off, while others bore traces of torture, arrows having been born into their private parts while still living."

Cheyenne Chief Two Moon later described the battle to historian Hamlin Garland. "The shooting was quick, quick. Pop, pop, pop. Very fast. Some of the soldiers were down on their knees, some standing. Officers all in front. The smoke was like a great cloud, and everywhere the Sioux went dust rose like smoke. We shoot, we ride fast, we shoot again. Soldiers drop, and horses fall on them."

Yellow Hair, General George Armstrong Custer, was no more.

CALAMITY JANE – FRONTIERSWOMAN AND INDIAN SCOUT, OR BRAGGART AND PROSTITUTE?

Calamity Jane could best be described as a man, trapped in a woman's

body. She could out drink, out ride, out shoot, and cuss louder, and nastier than any man alive. An article in *The Black Hills Daily Times* said she looked like the "result of a cross between the gable end of a fireproof and a Sioux Indian." She stood nearly six-foot-tall, had stringy, unwashed hair, and a rough, weather-beaten appearance. When asked to describe her, most acquaintances would say she had a tall, muscular build, more male than female, and often dressed in buckskins and leather britches, but when she did wear a dress—still appeared more masculine, than feminine.

Whiskey was her downfall. A July 7, 1877, article in the *Cheyenne Daily Leader* said "she is lifted high up into the heavens on the wings of a snifter and in the next plunged into a sea of unutterable gloom…as a female holy terror, she has no living superior, and her worst enemies will not deny that she is an able drinker."

She was born Martha Jane Cannary in Pleasanton, Missouri on May 1, 1852. Her family migrated to Virginia City, Montana in 1865. It was a five-month journey by wagon train. Martha Jane said, "The greater portion of my time was spent in hunting along with the men and hunters of the party, in fact, I was all the time with the men when there was excitement and adventure to be had."

Her mother died at Black Foot, Montana in 1866, shortly after they arrived. In the spring of that year, the family moved farther west to Salt Lake City, Utah. Her father passed away in 1867. That's when the story of Calamity Jane began.

Martha Jane moved her five siblings to Fort Bridger in Wyoming Territory and started doing odd jobs. Most biographies say she cleaned, cooked, worked as a dance hall girl, and possibly, as a prostitute.

She became a scout for General George Armstrong Custer in 1870, working out of Fort Russell, Wyoming. Calamity said, "when I joined Custer I donned the uniform of a soldier. It was a bit awkward at first, but I soon got to be perfectly at home in men's clothes."

She fought Indians in Arizona during the winter of 1871, returned to Fort Sanders, Wyoming in 1872, and in 1873 headed out to fight in the Nursey Pursey Indian outbreak. This campaign earned her the nickname "Calamity Jane."

The way Martha Jane told the story, she was stationed at Goose Creek, Wyoming. The soldiers were on the trail for several days squashing an Indian uprising in which six soldiers in her company died. Indians ambushed the group as they returned to the post, Captain Egan got shot. Jane watched him sway, and nearly fall out of his saddle. She rushed back, blasting Indians with her rifle, grabbed the captain, and tossed him across her saddle as they rode to safety.

When he recovered, Captain Egan told her, "I name you Calamity Jane, the heroine of the plains." A 1903 article published in *The Wide World Magazine* words it a little differently. Egan told her, "a man [would be] unusually lucky to have such heroines as Jane in times of calamity."

After this, Calamity says she was ordered north with General Crook to join Generals Miles, Terry, and Custer at the Little Big Horn. Fortunately, or unfortunately, however you look at it, Calamity "contracted a severe illness" swimming her pony across the Platte River near Fort Fetterman. Otherwise, she would likely have died with Custer on the Little Big Horn.

That's the story told by Martha Jane Cannary. The truth might be a little different. Captain Jack Crawford, the chief of scouts for General Crook, during that campaign, wrote an article for *The Journalist* on March 5th, 1904. Crawford said, Martha "was not with the command at any time." The only time General Crook recognized her was to "order her out of camp when he discovered she was a camp follower." The meaning was clear— she was a *prostitute*, not a scout.

Captain Jack Crawford also disputed the story about how Calamity Jane got her name. He says, "Now I was with Captain Egan and his White Horse Troop and helped patrol the roads between Ft. Laramie and Red Canon, and no such fight ever took place, nor was Captain Egan wounded." Of course, the article was published a year after her death, so Calamity had no chance to dispute the facts.

When she recovered, Calamity made her way to Fort Laramie where she hooked up with Wild Bill Hickok. They headed for Deadwood in June 1876, and Jane was soon working as a Pony Express rider delivering mail between Deadwood and Custer riding through the "roughest trails in the Black Hills."

One time, when she was riding the mail, Calamity was chased by two Sioux Indians. While jumping her horse across a small creek, the horse broke his leg. With the Indians, almost upon her and only two bullets in her gun, Calamity jumped off her horse, unloaded one ball into his brains to end his suffering. She shot one of the Indians dead, and scared the other into surrendering, then marched him off to jail in Deadwood.

Wild Bill was shot and killed by Jack McCall on August 2nd, 1876 while playing poker at Nuttall and Mann's Saloon in Deadwood. When she heard about the shooting, Calamity said she chased "the assassin and found him at Shurdy's Butcher Shop grabbed a meat cleaver and made him throw up his hands."

Again, the truth was a little different.

McCall was taken prisoner, tried by a jury made up mainly of miners, and acquitted. He made his way to Wyoming and was arrested again for the murder of Wild Bill. The second trial held in Yankton, Dakota Territory, found McCall guilty of murder. The jury sentenced him to death, and he was hanged on March 1st, 1877.

Calamity began her climb to national fame shortly after Wild Bill's death. She appeared alongside of Deadwood Dick in issue number one of *Beadle's Half-Dime Library*. Several years later she grabbed top billing in a serial published by *Street and Smith's Weekly,* titled *Calamity Jane: Queen of the Plains.*

Calamity says she rejoined the 7th Cavalry in 1877 and helped build Fort Meade, and the town of Sturgis, Colorado. The next year she left the army and spent the better part of a year prospecting around Rapid City. When mining didn't pan out, she returned to Colorado and started ranching on the Yellowstone. A few years later Calamity found herself in California, and then El Paso, Texas where she married Clinton Burk. In her autobiography, *Life and Adventures of Calamity Jane, by Herself,* she said it was time to settle down.

The couple soon left Texas. They headed to Boulder, Colorado, where they ran a hotel. Calamity signed a contract with Kohl and Middleton in

1895, that took her to *The Palace Museum* in Minneapolis, Minnesota. It didn't take her long to lose that job for being drunk and disorderly on stage. Calamity appeared at the Pan American Exposition in 1901, and some say later, in some of Buffalo Bill's Wild West Shows, but Captain Jack Crawford says "another certainty is that she never saw the original Buffalo Bill."

Like most things in the life of Calamity Jane, distinguishing truth from fiction is nearly impossible. Newspapers printed tall tales, false interviews, and made up drivel; dime novelists portrayed Calamity as a hard-drinking, fast shooting, Hellcat of the west. And, by all accounts Calamity, Jane did everything she could to encourage the stories.

She died in early August of 1903 at the Calloway Hotel in Terry, South Dakota, most likely from alcohol complications. They buried Martha Jane next to Wild Bill at Mount Moriah Cemetery.

CHARLES JULIUS GUITEAU - INSANITY, ASSASSINATION, AND CELEBRITY

 Most Americans alive today have never heard of Charles Julius Guiteau.

It's a sign of our love-hate relationship with history. Guiteau was a drifter and failed lawyer who hailed from Freeport, Illinois. He made his way to Washington, DC, with delusions of receiving a public appointment, possibly even of becoming president.

Instead, he wound up assassinating President James Garfield and spawned a trial that enthralled the nation during the closing days of 1881.

Guiteau testified: "I was in my bed … and I was thinking over the political situation, and the idea flashed through my brain that if the President was out of the way everything would go better … the only way to unite the two factions of the Republican party, and save the Republic from going into the hands of the rebels and Democrats, was to quickly remove the President."

Later, during his trial, Guiteau told Judge Cox, "I presume I shall live to be President. Some people think I am as good a man as the President (Chester A. Arthur) now.

"Providence and I saved the nation, and why should I not be a hero and the equal of Washington, Lincoln, and Grant?"

. . . .

It was a crazy mixed up summer.

A drifter from Illinois made his way to Washington determined to kill the President of the United States. Fate seemed as if it would intervene to keep Guiteau from his task, but on the morning of July 2nd, 1881, the shooter seized his opportunity.

The place was the Baltimore and Potomac Railway Station in Washington. Guiteau said he "was about three or four feet from the door. I stood five or six feet behind him, right in the middle of the room, and as he was walking away from me, I pulled out the revolver and fired. He straightened up and threw his head back and seemed to be perfectly bewildered. He did not appear to know what struck him. I looked at him; he did not drop; I thereupon pulled again. He dropped his head, seemed to reel, and fell over."

White smoke and powder filled the area around the fallen president.

By some miracle, Garfield didn't die. He lingered on the brink of death throughout the summer of 1881. Several times, it appeared as if he would recover, but the president passed away on September 19th, 1881.

. . . .

Guiteau's erratic actions during his trial made him a media sensation.

He pled not guilty on three counts.

- Insanity. "It was God's act, not mine."
- Garfield's doctors killed him, not Guiteau. It was a simple case of malpractice.
- Lack of jurisdiction.

The trial lasted over three months.

Guiteau's brother-in-law, Charles J. Scoville, acted as counsel for the defense. He dismissed the last two pleas and focused on the "insanity" defense.

On the witness stand, Guiteau testified, "It was on the inspiration of the Deity. I never would have shot the president on my own personal account."

Later he was asked, "You did not succeed in the Divine will?"

He responded, "I think the doctors finished the work."

Recent studies tend to favor the malpractice defense. Doctors were unaware of the need for proper sanitation. They moved from patient to patient, without washing their hands, or sanitizing medical equipment, spreading germs and infections as they went.

Doctors believed a bullet lodged in the president's torso. Without X-ray machines or other modern diagnostic equipment, doctors used the only tools available to them at the time. They jammed their dirty fingers and instruments into the wound, probing deeper and deeper, in their attempts to find the lost bullet.

Guiteau ranted and raved like a madman during the trial—pacing, and spouting crazy ideas—that he was a messenger from God. God inspired him to remove the president.

Reporters ate it up. Reports of the trial spread across the nation.

The questions continued:

"Do you think it was the Will of God that you should kill the president?"

"I believe that it was His will that he should be removed, and I was appointed the agent to do it."

"Did he give you a commission in writing?"

"No sir."

"Did he give it to you audibly?"

"No sir."

"He did not come to you as a vision in the night?"

"I do not get my inspiration in that way."

The testimony dragged on for months. Each side hauled doctors and lawyers before the court. The defense, to demonstrate Guiteau was certifiably insane. The prosecution, to show it was all an elaborate scam.

In the end, the jury returned a guilty verdict after only twenty minutes of deliberation.

When he received his death sentence, Guiteau screamed, "My blood will be upon the heads of the jury; don't you forget it.

"God will avenge this outrage!"

. . . .

Charles Julius Guiteau was hung by the neck until dead on June 30, 1882. After a half hour of dangling by a rope, his body was taken down and placed in a waiting coffin.

Thus, ended Guiteau's fifteen minutes of fame.

WESTERN BAD MEN

I don't know about you, but when I think about gunfighters, I reflect on the classic western showdown, where two men meet on the street. Faces poke out from behind windows. Heads pop up from behind benches and chairs, hoping to catch a glimpse. The two men stare each other down. They unsnap their holsters and begin walking slowly towards each other. They take one last draw on their cigarette and toss the smoldering butt to the ground. Their eyes squint in the glaring sun. They draw. One, or both, of the shooters, fall dead, as the crowd rushes out to get a glimpse of the body.

Obviously, I've watched too many westerns.

. . . .

For over 150 years, the image of western bad men has thrilled readers and filled movie screens. Who hasn't heard of Jesse James, the Dalton Brothers, Black Bart, or Belle Starr? They are as much a part of American folklore as George Washington, Abraham Lincoln, and Theodore Roosevelt.

There's something about the west that brought out the best and the worst in humanity. The funny thing is a cult following has developed around many of these bandits making them out to be something they weren't.

The story is Joaquin Murrieta was just an average guy who moved from Mexico to California, hoping to strike it rich during the gold rush. What he discovered instead, was a big sign, that read "No Mexicans Allowed." His supporters say that because of the Foreign Claim Tax he was forced off his land, and into a life of outlawry. And, then to support that claim, a whole legend has been built up about how he stole from the rich and shared his wealth with poor Mexican families. The only problem is—the facts don't support that interpretation. Murrieta and his gang of outlaws specialized in robbing poor Chinese immigrants. The only people they shared with were themselves.

The same stories developed around Jesse James. Legend has it Jesse only stole from wealthy bankers and railroad men. The reason he could disappear into thin air after pulling a bank job or train robbery was because he shared the booty with poor Missouri families. As with Murrieta, that probably never happened. Jesse James was a thief. He stole money wherever he could get his hands on it. He robbed stagecoaches, banks, trains, and you-name-it. And, as far as just robbing the rich, not so. During most of their train and stage robberies, the James-Younger Gang collected money and jewelry from the passengers, as well as the booty from the express car.

Bob Ford was another interesting character. He was a gunfighter, a robber want-to-be, who along with his brother, Charlie, got into Jesse James's good graces, and then shot him in the back. Several years later he met the same fate in a dancehall in Colorado.

My personal favorite is Black Bart, the gentlemen robber of the west. Bart only robbed Wells Fargo stagecoaches. He always asked the drivers to "Please throw down the box." Of course, he backed his request up with a double-barreled shotgun. Bart singlehandedly pulled twenty-eight stage coach robberies over an eight-year period without ever firing a shot. After his capture, he served his time then disappeared completely off the radar after his release.

And, last, but not least—there's Belle Starr, one of the worst female robbers on record. Belle called her pistols her "babies." She ruled an outlaw kingdom based out of her home in Indian Territory. Belle lived by the gun, and she died by the gun.

JOAQUIN MURRIETA
CALIFORNIA BANDIT

Most of what we know about Joaquin Murrieta is pure horse-hockey. A California journalist, John Rollin Ridge (Yellow Bird), created the legend most people know as Joaquin Murrieta in his 1854 book, *The Life, and Adventures of Joaquin Murieta.*

The book makes Murrieta out to be a modern-day Robin Hood, forced into outlawry by racist whites. He turned to stealing horses, robbery, and murder—taking from the rich, and distributing his plunder among poor Mexican families.

The only problem is there's no evidence to support this.

The few facts we know about Murrieta is he came to California, from old Sonora, Mexico sometime in 1850, to try his luck in the goldfields. It is likely his wife, Rosa, several of her brothers, and his brother Carlos came with him.

They staked a claim near Hangtown and may have lost their property due to the Foreign Claim Tax (a penalty imposed on non-white miners to keep them out of California). Sometime in 1851 Joaquin Murrieta joined his brother-in-law, Claudio Feliz's gang. That was his introduction to outlawry, and he joined the band in robbing and murdering lone travelers. Claudio's band terrorized the mine fields for two years until they were recognized as they tried to rob the John Kottinger Rancho near Pleasanton. Shortly after that, they robbed a native Californian, rather than their usual prey of Chinese immigrants. The gang was tracked down, and Claudio was killed fighting off his pursuers.

Joaquin Murrieta assumed leadership of the band after the death of Claudio Feliz. Manual Garcia, known as Three Finger Jack, served as his headman. Together, they initiated a six-month reign of terror in Calaveras County beginning in early 1853.

Governor John Bigler organized the California Rangers on May 11th, 1853. They were an elite group, led by former Texas Ranger, Harry Love, and charged with taking down Murrieta's band, known as *The Five Joaquin's*. The gang was made up of Joaquin Murrieta, Joaquin Botellier, Joaquin Carillo, Joaquin Ocomorenia, Joaquin Valenzuela, and Three Finger Jack.

The Five Joaquin's rustled 100 horses, stole over $100,000 in gold, and killed between 19 and 22 men (most of them Chinese).

Harry Love and the California Ranger's received a break in July of 1853 when they captured Jesus Feliz, a brother of Claudio Feliz. He ratted Murrieta out and gave the Ranger's the location of his hideout.

A story published in the *Los Angeles Herald*, said Love's posse ambushed Murrieta and Three Finger Jack while they were in camp near Cantua Creek. Jack was shot and killed immediately along with several other members of the gang. Joaquin jumped on a horse and fled for his life. He was shot in the wrist and fell off his horse. When he realized, he was outgunned Murrieta dropped his gun and threw up his hands. The posse disregarded his attempt to surrender and filled Murrieta with lead.

After the posse killed Murrieta, Love had them chop off his head and Three Finger Jack's signature hand. They preserved them in jars of whiskey and brought them back to Governor Bigler as proof they had earned their reward of $1,000. State legislators were so happy; they awarded the posse an additional $5,000 reward the next year.

Once they collected their reward, Harry Love, and the California Rangers, displayed the jar containing Murrieta's head around the Mariposa mining camps for $1.00 a peek. The head eventually made its way to the back bar at the Golden Nugget Saloon and was destroyed in the San Francisco earthquake of 1906.

Several years after his death Murrieta's sister claimed the head in the jar wasn't Murrieta's. She said it didn't have a distinctive scar on the cheek.

BILLY THE KID – NEW MEXICO OUTLAW, GUNFIGHTER, AND CATTLE THIEF

Charles Siringo, in his *History of Billy the Kid*, portrayed Billy as a

crazed psycho killer who made his first kill at age twelve. Siringo said, Billy snuck off to Fort Union, New Mexico, where he gambled with the black soldiers. A "black nigger" cheated him. Billy shot the man dead. Not long after that, he stabbed a man three times in a saloon fight, then ran out of the establishment with blood dripping from his right hand.

Siringo blamed the murder on Billy's violent temper, but Sheriff Pat Garrett, the man who would eventually track Billy down, and kill him, said just the opposite. Garrett said people often talked about the look in Billy's eye, and his temper just before he killed, but *the Kid* wasn't like that. Garrett said, Billy ate "and laughed, drank and laughed, talked and laughed, fought and laughed and killed and laughed."

The only picture we have of Billy the Kid doesn't do him justice. He looks more like a mental defective with a lopsided face than someone often described as a lady's man. Billy stood five foot, eight inches tall, weighed about 140 pounds, and had a stringy muscular build. His hair was a sandy brownish-blond, and the one personality trait that always stuck out about the Kid was his sense of humor.

In other circumstances, he might have been a politician or a business mogul, but in the old west, he was a gunman and one of the best at his trade.

We don't know much about the Kid's early life. He may have been born in New York, or in Indiana, but there is no evidence to favor either state. He was born William Henry McCarty, Jr., but the name he used in New Mexico was William H. Bonney.

His first *real kill* occurred sometime after he turned sixteen. Frank "Windy" Cahill, the blacksmith at Fort Grant, got a kick out of bullying and pushing Billy around. One day he pushed him a little too far and began chasing and swearing at him. Finally, he knocked him to the ground and started to pummel his face. Billy was no fool. He knew he couldn't out fight Cahill, so he pulled his gun, and shot him dead. The coroner's inquest labeled the killing a homicide, and Billy hit the trail one step ahead of the law.

Billy reappeared in Lincoln County, New Mexico Territory, sometime in 1877. It was about this time he changed his name to William H. Bonney and began working for the Coe-Saunders ranch. That move placed him smack-dab in the center of the Lincoln County War.

The Lincoln County War began in the summer of 1876 but started to heat up in the spring of 1877. John Chisum was the *Cattle King of New Mexico*. He ran 40,000 to 80,000 head of cattle letting them range over a 200-square mile area. The smaller ranchers accused Chisum of swallowing up their livestock and placing the Chisum brand on them. Chisum claimed just the opposite. He said the small ranchers cut cattle out of his herds and sold them at the army posts for a quick profit.

Alex McSween was a prominent Lincoln County lawyer and ally of John Chisum. He first worked as a lawyer for Murphy and Dolan but later switched allegiances to work as an attorney for John Chisum. Murphy and Dolan claimed McSween had been embezzling money from them.

John Tunstall was a wealthy Englishman who was convinced by Alex McSween that Lincoln County was ripe for the picking. Tunstall bought a ranch on the Rio Feliz and set up a store and bank in the town of Lincoln. In doing so, he allied himself with the Chisum faction.

Lawrence Murphy and James Dolan ran the Murphy-Dolan store just down the street from Tunstall's new store. They'd enjoyed a monopoly on business in Lincoln since Murphy started the business in 1869, and because of that charged the local ranchers exorbitant prices for their goods. When Tunstall opened his store, and charged lower prices, it began to steal business away from the Murphy-Dolan store.

Things soon turned violent with each side employing hired guns to get their way.

In February of 1878, Deputy Sheriff William Morton, and his posse began rounding up horses owned by Tunstall and McSween. Morton claimed Tunstall pulled his gun, so he shot him off his horse. Pat Garrett said, Tom Hill rode up to Tunstall, placed his shotgun to his head, and "scattered his brains over the ground."

Richard M. Brewer, Tunstall's ranch foreman, was sworn in as a special constable in Lincoln, and his posse, known as the Regulators, rode off in search Tunstall's killers. They captured Morton and Baker on March 6th but reported them killed in an escape attempt on March 9th. The Regulators later ambushed and killed Sheriff William Brady, and his deputy, Fred Waite, on the main street of Lincoln.

Violence continued to rage throughout the spring and summer of 1878. New Mexico Governor Lew Wallace (a former Civil War general, and the author of *Ben Hur*) offered an amnesty for any man involved in the

Lincoln County War who wasn't currently under indictment. Billy sent Wallace a letter offering to testify in return for an amnesty. Governor Wallace and the Kid met in Lincoln in March of 1879 to negotiate for Billy's testimony. The story is Billy met Wallace with a six-shooter in one hand and a Winchester 73 rifle in the other.

By the terms of their deal, Billy was be arrested for a short period. When he was done testifying, they would set him free. The bargain wasn't kept, and the Kid soon escaped. His life remained uneventful for the next year and a half. He stole a few horses and rustled some cattle. The only standout event during this period was his gun battle with Joe Grant, a gunfighter wannabe. The story is Grant went on a wild bender at Hargrove's Saloon and grabbed a gun from one of Billy's compadres. Billy got ahold of the gun, and set it to an empty chamber, then egged Grant into a fight. When Grant pulled his gun, it clicked on an empty cylinder, and Billy shot him dead.

Pat Garrett was elected sheriff of Lincoln County in November of 1880 and set out with a posse to chase down Billy. The kid was outgunned and surrendered to Garrett. He was turned over to the United States Marshal Charles Conklin in Santa Fe, New Mexico, on December 27, 1880. His trial was held at Mesilla, New Mexico, in March of 1881. Billy, the Kid, was sentenced to be hanged on May 13th, 1881 for the killing of Sheriff William Brady.

Garrett locked Billy up in the old Murphy-Dolan store in Lincoln. On the evening of April 28th, Billy overpowered Deputy J. W. Bell on the stairs outside of the prison snatched his gun and shot him dead. Inside the jailhouse, he grabbed Pat Garrett's rifle from his office and laid in wait for Deputy Marshal Robert Olinger. After killing Olinger, Billy stole a horse and galloped out of town.

On July 14th, Garrett received word the Kid was holed up in the abandoned ruins of Fort Sumner, and he rode off to bring him in. In Garrett's account of Billy's death published in his book, *The Authentic Life of Billy the Kid*, he said he went to the ranch of Peter Maxwell looking for the Kid.

Garrett was in Maxwell's bedroom questioning him on the whereabouts of the Kid when Billy stumbled in with a six-shooter in one hand, and a meat cleaver in the other. It was dark. At first, Billy didn't realize there was anyone in the room with Maxwell.

Maxwell whispered, "That's him!"

The Kid jumped back, "raised his pistol, a self-cocker, within a foot of my breast. Retreating rapidly across the room, he cried: 'Quien es?' 'Quien es?' All this occurred in a moment. Quickly as possible I drew my revolver and fired, threw my body aside, and fired again. The second shot was useless; the kid fell dead. He never spoke. A struggle or two, a little strangling sound as he gasped for breath, and the Kid was with his victims."

JESSIE JAMES AND THE JAMES-YOUNGER GANG

Jesse and Frank James are perhaps the best-known bandits of the old west. They fought with Confederate raiders William Quantrill and "Bloody Bill" Anderson during the Civil War. In October of 1864, Frank traveled to Kentucky with Quantrill. Jesse rode off to Texas with Archie Clement.

After the war, they returned to their homes in Clay County, Missouri, and shortly after that turned outlaw.

The James-Younger Gang committed their first bank robbery at Liberty, Missouri on February 13th, 1866. "A dozen desperadoes armed to the teeth, and superbly mounted, swooped down on the city." They overpowered the cashiers at the Clay County Savings Bank and forced them to stash over $72,000 into their saddle-bags. While it's unlikely Jesse was involved in this robbery (he was recovering from a severe chest wound he received at the end of the war), Frank James, Cole Younger, and Archie Clement are said to have participated.

Just after noon on December 7th, 1869, Frank and Jesse James robbed the Daviess County Savings Association in Gallatin, Missouri. Two horsemen rode up to the door of the Daviess County Savings Bank. Jesse jumped off of his horse and went into the bank. He ordered the cashier, John W. Sheets, to put all of the money in a bag. When Sheets finished, Jesse placed a gun to his head and put a bullet in his brain, and another in his heart. While they were escaping one of the riders slipped off of his horse, and got his foot caught in his stirrup. The horse dragged him for nearly fifty feet. The other rider came back to help him, amidst a flurry of gunfire from the townspeople. The two men made good their escape with about $700.

Speculation has it Jesse mistook Sheets for Samuel Cox, the leader of the troops who killed "Bloody Bill" Anderson towards the end of the Civil War. The more likely explanation is he didn't give a damn. Jesse murdered Sheets for the fun of it.

Six men rode up to the Ocobock Brothers Bank in Corydon, Iowa on June 13th, 1871. Three men entered the bank. Three stood watch outside. The robbers inside the bank bound cashier Ted Wock, hand, and foot, and made off with nearly $9,000 in cash, gold, and stamps. As they rode out of town, they paused at a political rally where Henry Clay Dean was speaking. The bandits took a few moments to brag about the robbery, and rode off, leaving the townspeople bewildered.

The Pinkerton Detective Agency, said the James Gang switched tactics and began robbing stagecoaches after the Corydon bank robbery. They made a good job of it—working southern Missouri and Arkansas, particularly in the area around Hot Springs.

The James Gang pulled their first train robbery at Adair, Iowa on July 21st, 1873. Nine men including Jesse and Frank James, Cole, Jim, Bob, and John Younger, Clell Miller, Bill Chadwell, and Charlie Pitts derailed a section of track outside of the Adair Depot just after 8:30 PM. The gang expected the train to stop. Instead, the engine and two baggage cars were thrown from the track when engineer John Rafferty slammed on the air brakes. Rafferty was crushed and killed by the engine; fireman Dennis Foley survived with serious injuries.

Four of the robbers went to the Express car and ordered the agent, John Burgess to open the safe. The gang was disappointed when they discovered the safe contained only $2,000 so they proceeded to rob the passengers. While the men inside the passenger cars collected cash and jewelry from the passengers, the robbers outside fired their guns into the air to scare the passengers.

When they finished robbing the passengers, the robbers jumped on their horses and made a clean getaway.

The James Gang's next target was the Iron Mountain Railroad at Gad's Hill, Missouri. The *Salt Lake Herald* published on April 16th, 1882, said the boys "took possession of the station, switched a train on the side track, and at their leisure…stripped the passengers of their surplus wealth and robbed the express car of $11,500."

The gang put out a signal for the train to stop and started a small brush fire to ensure they would catch the train crew's attention. As the train slowed down, five masked, heavily armed robbers hopped on the train. Engineer William Wetton and Conductor C. A. Alford were taken prisoner, along with the rest of the crew. One of the bandits rode up and down among the cars, and fired his guns into the air, to keep the passengers inside cowed. After they broke into the safe and stole all the money from it, the robbers began walking up and down in the passenger cars and gathered up all of the loot they could.

As the gang got ready to leave, Jesse James handed engineer William Wetton a note for the press. It read:

The most daring robbery on record

The Southbound train on the Iron Mountain railroad was boarded here this evening by five heavily armed men and robbed of _____ dollars. The robbers arrived at the station a few minutes before the arrival of the train and arrested the agent and put him under a guard and then threw the train on the switch.

The robbers are all large men, none of them under six feet tall. They were all masked and started in a southerly direction after they had robbed the express. They were all mounted on fine blooded horses. There's a hell of an excitement in this part of the country.

The Northfield Minnesota bank raid on September 7th, 1876, was the farthest the James-Younger Gang had ever traveled from their home base in Missouri.

An article published in the *Salt Lake Herald* on April 16th, 1882, said "On the afternoon of the 7th, the desperadoes dashed into the town, shooting their revolvers and halting in front of the Northfield bank…The citizens on the street realized what was going on and opened fire on the robbers. Chadwell was shot from his horse…and, in just a few minutes…Clell Miller was also killed. Jim Younger had a bullet in his mouth, and Frank James one through his left leg."

Here's the way it all happened. Three of the robbers entered the bank; the rest remained outside to keep watch. Cashier Haywood refused to open the safe. Teller Bunker was shot in the shoulder by Bob Younger as he attempted to escape through the front door. Frank James shot and killed

Haywood, saying it was "a warning to those bank cashiers to open up when we ask them."

Once the shooting inside the bank started, the gunfire outside picked up. The townspeople kept up an intense fire from behind doors and windows. "Two of [the robbers] fell dead from their saddles. A third was so sorely wounded that he nearly fell, and was forced to beg his companions not to desert him. One of them got on the horse with him and held him during the retreat."

Clell Miller and Bill Chadwell died at Northfield, Charlie Pitts got shot up and killed by the posse during the pursuit.

The posse caught up with the gang as they crossed Lake Hanska Slough. Sheriff Gilpin ordered the robbers to halt. They refused and retreated to the Watonwan River amidst heavy gunfire. The posse continued to chase them into the river and onto the palm brush on the south side of the river.

One robber threw up his hands and surrendered. He led the sheriff to where the rest of the gang was holed up. The *Mower County Transcript* on September 28th, 1876 reported, "Cole Younger and his brother were seen to fall and were heard groaning, and the other brother, wounded at Northfield, stepped out of the brush saying, 'Don't fire anymore, we are all shot to pieces.' Cole Younger and his brother were found lying together on the ground, badly wounded."

Jesse and Frank James headed off in a different direction and made good on their escape. It was the end of the James-Younger Gang. Jesse and Frank would later operate as the James Gang, but nothing they did was as spectacular as the great Northfield, Minnesota raid, or their earlier robberies.

Jesse James was shot and killed in his home on April 5th, 1882. Not long after that, Frank James began negotiations with Missouri Governor Crittenden to surrender. Frank asked for clemency, but Crittenden made no promises, other than that he would ensure Frank would receive a fair trial. He met Major Edwards at the Capitol in Jefferson City and was taken to meet with Governor Crittenden in the Executive Office where he surrendered his gun belt and gun to the Governor.

After several weeks in prison, Frank was acquitted of all charges against him and released. Unlike Cole Younger and his brothers, Frank James never had to serve any time in the penitentiary.

BOB FORD – "THE DIRTY LITTLE COWARD" WHO SHOT JESSE JAMES

"There was never a more cowardly and unnecessary murder committed in all America than this murder of Jesse James. It was done for money."

Evening Bulletin,

Maysville, Kansas

May 4, 1882

. . . .

Bob Ford is one of the most interesting and least understood characters of the old west. Ford was an outlaw want-to-be who teamed up with Jesse James sometime in 1881. From the sound of it, Bob Ford didn't participate in any of the robberies committed by the James Gang. His brother, Charley Ford, rode with Jesse James and participated in the Blue Cut train robbery near Glendale, Missouri.

The original James Gang had dwindled to just Jesse by the end of 1881. Most of the Younger brothers were killed or imprisoned after the failed Northfield bank raid in 1876; several members left the gang in 1880 hoping to escape arrest. Frank James, moved to Lynchburg, Virginia, figuring it was time to go straight.

Jesse moved his family to St. Joseph, Missouri in November of 1881. Like Frank, he planned to give up the outlaw life, and settle down on a farm somewhere in Nebraska. But first, he needed one last score so that he could retire comfortably. That's where the Ford's came in. Jesse recruited them to assist with his final job—robbing the Platte City Bank. The week before they intended to complete the bank job, the Ford's moved in with Jesse and his family, masquerading as his cousins, Bob and Charley Johnson.

Unknown to Jesse, Bob Ford had a run-in with the law several months before this for killing Wood Hite. Rather than go to jail, he cut a deal with Sheriff James Timberlake, and Missouri Governor Thomas T. Crittenden, and offered to deliver Jesse James—dead, or alive. An article in the *Mexico Weekly Ledger* (Mexico, MO) published on April 6th, 1882, said Bob Ford's first meeting with Governor Crittenden took place at the St. James Hotel in Kansas City, Kansas, on February 22nd, 1882. Ford agreed to capture or kill Jesse James. In return, he would receive half of the $10,000 reward offered for Jesse James by the Railroads, and the State of Missouri, and a pardon for his part in the murder of Wood Hite.

Bob and Charley Ford weren't sure they'd get an opportunity to kill Jesse James. He was always heavily armed, and it was impossible to draw a weapon without him seeing it. On the morning of April 5th, 1882, Charley and Jesse spent several hours in the stable getting the horses ready for their raid on the Platte City Bank the next day.

It was a hot, humid morning. When Jesse and Bob returned to the house, Jesse looked at Bob, and said, "It's an awfully hot day." After that, he pulled off his coat and tossed it on a chair. "I guess I'll take off my pistols, for fear somebody will see them if I walk in the yard." He unbuckled his gun belt which contained two revolvers, a 45 caliber Smith and Wesson and a Colt. He then picked up a dusting cloth and climbed up on a chair to straighten some pictures.

Charley and Bob Ford grabbed their guns and quickly stepped between Jesse James and his pistols. The April 5th, 1882, edition of the *Evening Bulletin* (Maysville, KS) says, "Robert was the quickest of the two. In one motion, he had a long weapon to level with the muzzle no more than four feet from the back of the outlaw's head. The ball entered the base of the skull and made its way out through the forehead over the left eye."

Mrs. James was in the kitchen when she heard the shot. She rushed into the other room and found Jesse lying on the floor. The Ford's told her "it was an accident" as they slipped out of the door. Zee James "tried to wash away the blood that was coursing over [Jesse's] face from the hole in his forehead, but it seemed to her 'that the blood would come faster than she could wash it away.'"

Bob and Charley Ford rushed to the telegraph office to contact Sheriff Timberlake and Governor Crittenden. Jesse was dead, and they wanted to collect their reward. After notifying the officials, they surrendered to the local authorities.

Meanwhile, the coroner held an inquest. Jesse's wife identified the body and accused Bob and Charley Ford of murdering her husband. Mrs. Samuels, Jesse's mother, was brought in to identify the body. When asked, "Is that your son?" She replied, "It is. Would to God, it was not."

The Watchman and Southron reported on April 11th, 1882, "Governor Crittenden asserts positively that the body is that of Jesse James, and that his death was the result of an understanding between the authorities and Bob Ford." The Governor had fulfilled his campaign promise, to rid the state of Jesse James and his outlaw band.

The paper went on to say, "The Ford boys claim to have no object in view save to obtain the reward offered by Governor Crittenden for Jesse James, dead or alive. They had recently had two interviews with the

Governor at the St. James Hotel in Kansas City. The Governor was informed of their plan of action and approved it wholly.

"After the shooting, they promptly gave themselves up to authorities." Their trial was one of the swiftest on record. They were charged, pled guilty, sentenced to death, and pardoned—all in less than twenty-four hours. Things didn't go quite as they expected, though. The Governor promised the Ford's half of the ten-thousand-dollar reward. He later reneged on his promise, and the Ford's received less than five hundred dollars.

After the shooting, Bob and Charlie reenacted the killing in shows across the country and posed for pictures with gawkers and curio hunters. As that business slowed down the brothers moved on with their lives.

Charley Ford suffered from bouts of depression and bladder problems. He visited his parent's home in Kansas City in early May of 1884. The only relief he could get from the pain came from morphine, and he needed more and more of it to relieve the pain.

The St. Landry Democrat (Opelousas, LA) from May 24, 1884, reported his mother heard a gunshot, and "found Ford lying on his bed, breathing hard, while blood was oozing from his mouth and nostrils. The pistol, a large Colt five-shooter, was placed against his breast over the heart. It burned a large hole in his outer shirt."

Bob Ford's life also had its ups and downs. He wandered the west and tried his hand at odd jobs, gambling, and running saloons. Bob and a friend visited Cannon's Gambling House in Kansas City on Christmas Day, 1889. They played a game of Faro. A man started to talk crazy about how Bob had killed Jesse James. Then, "my abuser drew a knife from his pocket, and held my head back by my hair, and was about to draw the knife across my throat when my friend warded off the blow." The

Indianapolis Journal from December 26th, 1889 identified Bob's attacker as "Fats.".

Bob Ford quarreled with Deputy Watt Kelly over a girl in June of 1892. The *Sedalia Weekly Bazoo* (Sedalia, MO), June 14th, 1892, said "Kelly stepped into the dance hall. 'Bob,' he said, holding his weapon ready for action. Ford was standing with his back to Kelly scarcely five feet away. He turned and as he saw who called him his hand went for his six-shooter. But he had no chance on earth. The shotgun, heavily loaded with buckshot, did frightful work at so short a range. Ten whole charges struck full in Ford's neck tearing away his windpipe and jugular."

Bob Ford, the killer of Jesse James, died the same way he took Jesse's life—he was shot in the back by an assassin.

RISE AND FALL OF THE DALTON GANG

The Dalton Gang enjoyed a brief crime spree for about eighteen months beginning in early 1890. The funny thing is, before turning outlaw, the three Dalton brothers—Grat, Bob, and Emmett served as lawmen.

Their oldest brother, Frank Dalton, a United States Marshal, was shot and killed while trailing horse thieves through Oklahoma Territory in 1887. Brothers Bob, Grat, and Emmett, turned outlaw in early 1890 after they had trouble collecting their pay for some law enforcement work.

The Dalton Gang pulled off several train robberies between 1891 and 1892.

The first train they robbed was the Atlantic Express on February 6, 1891. The boys flagged the train down with a red lantern they grabbed from the station agent. As soon as the train stopped, two men wearing long black masks stepped onto the locomotive and covered the engineer with Colt revolvers.

They forced the fireman to grab his pick-axe and dragged him to the door of the express car. They told the agent inside to open the door. When he refused, they busted down the door. In the commotion, the robbers shot and killed fireman George Radliff. The agent jumped through the window and escaped into the brush. With him went any hope the Dalton's had of getting the money in the safe. In their hurry to rob the train, the gang forgot to bring dynamite to blow the safe.

Disgusted, they fired their guns into the air and rode away empty handed.

The Dalton's next robbery took place at Wharton Depot on the Cherokee Strip. Three men rode up to the station about 9:30 PM to meet the Texas Fast Express. Bob Dalton ordered the station agent to signal the train to stop. The gang pulled black masks over their faces before they boarded the train. The plan was the same as their previous robbery. They dragged the fireman to the Express car, pickaxe in hand, and forced him to break down the door.

The Dallas Morning News, May 11, 1891, said "It was a cool and successful piece of work done by experts. Not a shot was fired during the time and while the passengers knew what was going on no attempt was made to interfere. When a passenger thrust his head out of a window, he was promptly made to withdraw it."

The robbery at Red Rock Station occurred just before 10:00 PM on June 2nd, 1892. An article in the *Norman Transcript* on June 4th, 1892, said "Six masked men got on board and compelled fireman Rogers at the muzzle of Winchesters to break open the door of the express car with his pick, enter the car and smash the safe with a sledgehammer."

Another group of bandits made their way through the train gathering cash and valuables from the passengers. The robbers fired a volley through the windows of the passenger car as they rode away. The take from the Express car was slightly less than $2000.

The Dallas Morning News reported on July 16th, 1892. "One of the more daring train robberies on record took place last night at Adair, I. T. As the Missouri, Kansas, and Texas north-bound express train pulled into Adair station the train was held up and everything of value to be found was taken."

Nine gang members rode into Adair station that night. They took everything they could inside the station, tied up the station-master, and waited patiently on the platform for the train to arrive. It was a classic Dalton hold-up. They dragged the fireman to the express car with his pickaxe in hand. When express man George Williams refused to open the door, the gang fired shots through the car windows and threatened to dynamite the train. Williams opened the door, and they soon had all the valuables from the safe.

The *Dallas Morning News* added, "After a hard fight in which Chief Detective Kinney, Indian Policeman Laflore and two doctors, passengers on the train, were seriously wounded. None of the passengers coming to their aid and their revolvers being empty, they were forced to retreat into the train. A posse was hastily formed and returned to the scene of the robbery."

The take was estimated as high as $70,000 or $80,000.

Bob Dalton had this crazy idea.

He wanted to make the Dalton Gang more famous than Jesse James. The only problem was to do that he had to do something spectacular, something never tried before, something so bold, so daring the newspapers couldn't help but take notice.

When he told his brother Emmett what he wanted to do, Emmett thought he was nuts. Rob two banks, in the same town, at the same time, in a city everyone knew you in. It didn't make sense. The only reason

Emmett said he went along was, "he was damned if he did, and damned if he didn't." Even if he stayed out of it, he was sure the law would hunt him down.

The best account of the daring robbery was published in the *Coffeyville Journal* shortly after the robbery took place. "Between 9:30 and 10:00 on Wednesday morning, [the Dalton Gang] armed to the teeth and apparently disguised, rode boldly into [Coffeyville]."

The boys hitched their horses in an alley and quickly made their way to the two banks. Grat Dalton, Bill Powers, and Dick Broadwell entered the C. M. Condon Bank; Bob and Emmett Dalton hurried into the First National Bank.

Grat disguised himself with a black mustache and side whiskers. He ordered the clerk to hand over the cash, "and be quick about it." When one of the robbers told the cashier, C. M. Ball, to grab the money from the safe, he told them he couldn't—it was on a time lock, and no one could open it for another three minutes. By that time gunfire erupted outside the bank, and the robbers made a mad dash for the alley.

At the First National Bank, Bob Dalton disguised himself with a mustache and false goatee. "They covered the teller and cashiers with their Winchesters...and directed [the cashier] to hand over all the money in the bank." When they heard gunshots outside, Bob and Emmett hurried out the back door and opened fire. Lucius Baldwin, George Cubine, and Charles Brown fell dead.

By that time all five bandits were in the alley attempting to make their way to their horses. "A dozen men with Winchesters and shotguns made a barricade of some wagons. The robbers had to run the gauntlet of three hundred feet with their backs to the Winchesters in the hands of men who knew how to use them." A murderous fired poured through the alley for three minutes. "Three of the robbers were dead, and the fourth helpless." Dick Broadwell made it to his horse but was discovered dead on the ground about a half mile outside of town.

Emmett Dalton was the only member of the gang to survive. He was carried to Slosson's Drug Store, and later to Dr. Wells' office. There was a lot of talk about lynching him, but what probably saved his life more than anything, was the doctor didn't give him a chance in hell of surviving.

They carted the bodies of the dead gang members to the sheriff's office and placed them in four varnished black coffins where they were displayed and photographed so everyone would know what had happened. Some people touched the bodies as if that would make the experience more real. "Whenever Grat Dalton's right arm was lifted a little spurt of blood would jump from the round black hole in his throat."

The next day the town watched as the undertaker shooed flies away from the bodies, and nailed the lids on the caskets down. The coffins were planted two to a grave in Potter's Field.

The *Galveston Daily News* headline on October 6th, 1892 read, "The Dalton Gang has been exterminated—wiped off the face of the earth."

The only survivor, Emmett Dalton, received a life sentence in the Kansas State Penitentiary at Lansing. He was pardoned by Governor Ed Hoch in 1907 and lived until 1937. He later became a policeman, and actor, and wrote the story of his life, *When the Daltons Rode*, published in 1931.

"DYNAMITE DICK" CLIFTON – THE "MOST KILLED OUTLAW IN THE AMERICAN WEST."

Killing Dan "Dynamite Dick" Clifton was a popular pastime among Western newspaper editors who were quicker to print a story than to run a fact check. *Wikipedia* calls him "the most killed outlaw in the American West." There's no denying it. Just about every western newspaper published between 1895 and 1897 carried the gory details of Dynamite Dick "biting the big one"—going out with guns blazing, Winchester balls tearing through his body, leaving nothing but a blood-drenched carcass laying in the desert.

But, no sooner would you read about his death than he was robbing another bank, another train, or getting all shot up again. If he were alive today "Dynamite Dick" would be "Kenny" on *South Park*, or a famous victim in dozens of video games.

Legend has it Clifton got the name "Dynamite Dick" because he got a kick out of boring holes in his cartridges and filling them with dynamite. When they exploded, it made a hell of a ruckus and took a deadly toll on anyone or anything that crossed its path.

"Dynamite Dick" joined the Doolin-Dalton gang, or Wild Bunch, shortly after most of the Dalton Gang had been wiped out in the Coffeyville Bank raid.

One of the first jobs he pulled with the gang was the robbery of the Ford County bank in Spearville, Kansas on November 1st, 1892. Three men rode up to the bank at about 2 PM. One stayed outside to watch the horses; the other two men walked into the bank, revolvers at the ready. They put a gun to Cashier Baird's head, snatched up all the cash in sight, and walked out over $1700 richer. As they ran out of the bank and jumped on their horses, a group of citizens opened fire. Fifteen shots crashed around them; fortunately, no injuries occurred in the exchange.

The bandits headed south out of town with a posse hot on their trail. A running fight broke out on the trail, but after a few well-placed shots, the bandits made good on their getaway.

On June 10th, 1893, the gang robbed the Santa Fe Southern Express west of Cimarron, Kansas.

The *Meade County Globe* said, "Four masked robbers held up the California Express." The gang set up a danger signal about a half mile out of Cimarron. When the engineer stopped the train, two men, with revolvers drawn, jumped onto the train and forced the engineer to go with them to the express car. The express agent refused to open the door, so they blew it with dynamite. It's thought the boys made off with about $1,000 that time.

All hell busted loose in Southwest City, Missouri, in May of 1894, when the Doolin-Dalton gang robbed the bank there. By one account, over 100 shots were fired on Main Street as the gang made their getaway. Many townspeople said it "sounded like war times."

Seven men rode up to the bank about 3 PM. that afternoon. "Two of them were stationed on the sidewalk; three entered the bank with a sack and two others guarded the horses." Bill Doolin pulled a gun on cashier Snyder, and the bank owner, Mr. Ault. Another robber covered the rest of the employees, while the third crawled through the teller window, and began scooping up all of the money in sight.

A pitched fight broke out as the outlaws made good their escape. Four townsmen were wounded. Bill Doolin took several rounds of buckshot in the left temple close to the hairline but kept riding. "A posse was made up and started in pursuit," wrote a local paper, "but the robbers have a good lead and will probably get away."

Their take was $4,000.

The *San Francisco Call* proclaimed "Slaughter Kid and Dynamite Dick Riddled by Flying Buckshot." That was on May 3rd, 1895. A newspaper report said the "dead men were stretched out on two boards" at Spengle's undertaking house. Of course, they got some of the details wrong. They said, "Dynamite Dick" was Charlie Pierce, not Dan Clifton.

"Dynamite Dick" had "thirty buckshot in him, mostly in the right shoulder and side, although he had fully six shot in his stomach and as many in one foot. One Winchester bullet struck "Bitter Creek" in the forehead and tore out his brains at the back of his head, and the other hit his hand as he was pulling the trigger."

There was only one problem with that story.

A little later in May of the same year, "Dynamite Dick" and the Doolin-Dalton gang robbed the Rock Island Railroad at Dover. They got away with several thousand dollars from the express car, and some additional booty they took from the passengers.

Deputy Marshal Chris Madsen and seven posse members hit the trail in hot pursuit. "Tulsa Jack" Blake was killed during the chase. The other gang members got away, but their escape was short-lived. By the end of 1896, most of the Doolin-Dalton gang would be dead or in jail.

Bill Tilghman shot up Bill Raidler and put him in jail. Loss Hart killed Bill Dalton in an ambush outside of his wife's house. Charlie Pierce and "Bitter Creek" Newcomb got themselves shot full of holes by a couple of bounty hunters.

In 1896, Deputy F. M. Canton tracked "Dynamite Dick" down and put him behind bars. Two weeks later, on July 5th, 1896, Bill Doolin, "Dynamite Dick," and fourteen other prisoners busted out of the U. S. Prison at Guthrie, Oklahoma. They rushed one of the guards, seized two pistols and a Winchester, and forced the guards into the cages. Deputy Marshal Lightman and his posse rode off in hot pursuit.

On October 18th, 1896, six masked riders led by "Dynamite Dick" rode into the small town of Carney, Oklahoma, with their guns blazing. Two of the desperadoes pushed their way into the store of B. Fouts, and forced him and his son, to hand over the contents of the safe—about $800. After robbing them, the outlaws rode the two men a few miles out of town and tied them to a tree. While the Fouts were being terrorized and ridden out of the city, the other gang members ransacked the post office, hotel, and several smaller stores searching for anything of value. The entire time they were doing that the outlaws kept up a "horrible commotion" screaming and firing their guns into the air. When the boys finished with their fun, they rode out of town in three small groups.

Several months later, in December, "Dynamite Dick" used up another of his lives. Supposedly, a posse trailed him and another gang member,

Ben Cravens, to a spot three miles east of Blackwell, Indian Territory. The posse came upon the two men a little after daybreak.

The *Barbour County Index* said the Outlaws planned to rob the Bank of Blackwell about 9 AM that morning. Sheriff J. R. Cox received a tip the day before that "Dynamite Dick, " and Ben Cravens were hiding out at the house of a man named Hostler. He "organized a posse of seven good men in Blackwell, all of whom were splendidly equipped with arms, ammunition, and nerve." The posse challenged the outlaws to stop. Instead, they opened fire. "At the first round," fired by the posse, "Dynamite Dick fell before the bullet of a livery stable keeper named Lang…who used a .56 caliber Winchester rifle ball." Cravens was shot three times—once in the shoulder, another in the lung, and the third in the leg.

The headline in the *Wichita Daily Eagle* on December 5th, 1896, proudly proclaimed, "Dynamite Dick bites the dust." The editor of the *Shiner Gazette* dressed the story up a little, saying "bullets fell thick and hot on all sides for half an hour."

"Dynamite Dick" played out his final hand in 1897.

Even then, several stories circulated about the way in which he met his maker. The most published, said that Deputy Marshal George Lawson and Hess Bussey tracked Clifton to a cabin west of Checotha, Indian Territory.

The posse hollered for "Dynamite Dick" to surrender. As they did that, a woman and boy attempted to leave the cabin. The officers told them to set the cabin on fire—they refused and scurried back into the cabin.

Moments later "Dynamite Dick" burst through the door—a six-shooter in both hands, blasting at the marshals. Seconds later, "Dynamite Dick" fell dead for real.

Another version of the story says, the marshals tracked "Dynamite Dick" to a wooded area in Indian Territory. They soon discovered that a man answering to "Dynamite Dick's" description had been in the neighborhood for several weeks peddling whiskey. Post office inspector Houck and the two deputies waited in the woods near Blair Hill seeking clues. Two weeks later, they discovered the robbers had gone to Keokuk Falls to replenish their whiskey supplies but were set to return shortly.

When he got back, "Dynamite Dick" fired his Winchester into the air to let the locals know he had returned, and the hooch would soon be flowing freely. The marshals watched the drunken orgy all night from their perch in the woods.

The next morning, they moved in on "Dynamite Dick." He was leading a horse in one hand and held a rifle in the other. When the marshals challenged him to surrender, he raised his Winchester readying to fire. The marshals were too fast. Dynamite Dick took a bullet in his left arm, dropped his rifle, and ran into the woods.

The lawmen tracked him all day. That's when they located him in the house with the women and the boy. The deputies ordered him to drop his guns and come out, or they would fire the cabin. At that point, "Dynamite Dick" decided he'd rather go out in a blaze of glory. He came to the door of the house armed with a pistol and a shotgun and began firing at the officers.

The *Houston Daily Post* wrote, "After about twenty shots had been exchanged, Dynamite Dick fell dead, riddled with bullets."

"Dynamite Dick" had died his last death. Surprisingly, the stories this time were shorter and less spectacular than previous accounts of his death.

BLACK BART – CALIFORNIA'S GENTLEMAN BANDIT, STAGE COACH ROBBER, AND PO8

Black Bart was a dapper looking gentleman no one would ever have suspected of being a stagecoach robber. If you met him on the street, you would have taken him for a prosperous businessman. He wore only the finest hand-tailored clothes, stayed in the best hotels, sported a gold pocket watch, and wore a large diamond ring on his finger.

He stood ramrod straight, 5 feet, 8 inches tall, with gray hair, and a bushy mustache. And, when he robbed a stage, he was always on his best manners, asking the driver to "Please throw down the box."

Bart's first robbery took place on Funk Hill, a mountain pass in Calaveras County, California on July 26th, 1875. John Shine was driving the stage that day. Bart appeared from out of nowhere, wearing a long, soiled duster, his head covered with a flour sack, with holes cut for his eyes. Waving his shotgun as he talked, Bart asked the driver to "Please throw down the box."

John Shine looked around, not sure what to do. He could always make a run for it or grab his rifle. But, from the corner of his eyes, he caught a glimpse of six gun barrels pointing at him from a group of boulders.

Shine tossed down the box and drove away as commanded. As he left, he saw Bart hammering away at the box with a hatchet. When he got a little farther away, Shine stopped the coach and walked back to the site of the robbery. Shine found the broken strongbox. Upon further investigation, he realized the gun barrels he'd seen earlier, were nothing more than sticks positioned in the boulders to make it appear as if Bart was backed up by a gang of cutthroats.

Black Bart's fourth robbery occurred four miles outside of Fort Ross in Sonoma County, California, on August 3rd, 1877. He left a mysterious poem that gave him his name.

I've labored long and hard for bread
For honor and for riches
But on my corns too long you've tread
You fine haired Sons of Bitches
                    Black Bart, the PO8

Almost a year later he robbed another stage about one mile from Barry Creek Sawmill in Butte County, California, on July 25, 1878. A second poem was left in the strongbox.

Here I lay me down to sleep
To wait the coming morrow
Perhaps success perhaps defeat
And everlasting sorrow.
Let come what will, I'll try it on,
My condition can't be worse,
But if there's money in the box,

It's munny in my purse.

Black Bart, PO8

The press had a field day, printing and reprinting the poems, speculating upon their meaning.

During his eight-year crime spree, Bart robbed twenty-eight stagecoaches, all of them belonging to Wells Fargo. He never fired a shot in any of the robberies, and there is some question as to whether his shotgun was loaded, or not. Unlike Belle Starr, Jesse James, and the Younger Brothers, Bart never took a dime from any passengers. If any of them ever attempted to turn over their purse or possessions, Bart always told them Wells Fargo's gold was reward enough.

But, that doesn't mean the stagecoach drivers didn't fire at him. Bart jumped in front of a stagecoach driven by George W. Hackett on July 13, 1882. Hackett grabbed his rifle, and let loose a flurry of bullets. Bart took off running, like a chicken with his head cut off as he scooted towards the trees. One of the bullets grazed his head leaving a mark he would carry for the rest of his life.

Bart's last robbery occurred near the spot where he pulled his first job. Reason E. McConnell was driving the stagecoach up Funk Hill. Just as he rounded the bend of Yaqui Gulch, a hooded stranger jumped in front of him—shotgun in hand.

Bart requested McConnell to "Please throw the box down." McConnell replied that he couldn't. The stagecoach company bolted the box to the floorboards of the coach.

Bart ordered the driver to get off the coach and put rocks under the wheels so that the stagecoach wouldn't roll backward. Then he had McConnell unhitch the horses and start walking away. McConnell testified as he walked away, he could see the bandit whacking away at the box with a hatchet.

As he left McConnell met up with Jimmy Rolleri, a passenger, he'd let off the stage earlier so he could do some hunting. They made their way back to the stagecoach and fired at Bart as he ran into the woods. McConnell and Rolleri hitched the horses up and made their way back to town. Later they escorted a team of Wells Fargo detectives to the scene of the robbery.

The detectives scoured the area and found a small valise. One of the items they discovered inside of it eventually proved to be Bart's undoing. It was a linen handkerchief with the laundry mark FXO7.

Back at Wells Fargo headquarters Detective James Hume assigned Harry Morse to check with each of the 91 laundries in San Francisco. A week into the search Phineas Ferguson at Biggs California Laundry recognized the handkerchief. He directed Morse to Thomas C. Ware who ran a local tobacco shop. Ware identified Bart as Charles Boles and gave the detective his home address. A few days later, Morse returned to ask more questions. As the two men talked, Ferguson noticed Boles walking down the street, and offered to introduce him to Morse.

Morse told Bart he had an interest in mining and struck up a conversation as they walked. He invited Bart into his office at Wells Fargo. That's where they met Detective James Hume.

Bart played it cool at first. He didn't say anything about the robberies. Eventually, the detectives searched his room and found several handkerchiefs with the same laundry mark as the one found at the robbery site. They also found a duster like the one worn by the robber. Next, they had Reason McConnell and another driver, meet with Bart. Both men identified him as the robber.

With overwhelming evidence against him, Bart confessed and took the detectives to where he stashed the gold. At his trial, he pled guilty to just one stagecoach robbery and was sentenced to six years in San Quentin. He was a model prisoner and secured an early release for good behavior on January 21st, 1888.

Just over a month later he disappeared from the face of the earth never to be heard from again.

....

Here's what we know about Black Bart.

His real name was Charles E. Boles. He was born in England, and his parents moved to the United States when he was two years old. Charles and his cousin Dave headed off to California in 1849 hoping to strike it rich in the goldfields. They didn't have any luck and returned home the next year. Charles, his brother Robert, and Dave returned to California to try their luck again in 1852. Shortly after their arrival Dave and Robert took sick and died.

Charles threw in the towel and headed back east. He ended up in Illinois and married Mary Johnson in 1854. Charles farmed there until the start of the Civil War. During the war, he fought with the 116th Regiment of Illinois Infantry and participated in several campaigns including Sherman's March on Atlanta.

After the war, he returned home to Mary and the kids in Illinois, but he soon grew restless and struck off for the gold fields in Montana. He staked a claim there with Henry Roberts near Deer Creek. Not long after they set up their claim, several gentlemen associated with Wells Fargo tried to buy their land. When they wouldn't sell, the men shut off the water flow to their sluices, and Charles was forced to abandon his claim.

Several years later Charles Boles turned to a life of crime, robbing only Wells Fargo Stagecoaches.

It should be noted Charles never admitted to being Black Bart, and the name he gave prison officials was Charles Bolton or T. Z. Spalding. His real name is known because during his imprisonment he wrote many letters home to his wife Mary in Illinois.

Scholars believe Boles chose the name Black Bart after the name of a character in a science fiction story written in 1871, The Case of Summerfield.

BELLE STARR

Belle Starr was "a sure shot and murderess, who never forgot an injury nor forgave a foe." She said she never killed a man she didn't have to, adding, "Wouldn't you kill rather than to be killed?"

....

Belle Starr was born Myra Belle Shirley on February 3rd, 1846 in Carthage, Missouri. Her father was a Confederate sympathizer. Her brother rode with Quantrill's Raiders. As a young girl, Belle carried messages for her brother, and at one time or another, met up with Jesse James and the Younger brothers.

Rumors persist about an affair with Cole Younger, but the chances that it happened are exceedingly slim. She did marry his cousin, Bruce Younger in 1880, but that union lasted only a few weeks. In 1866 Belle married James Reed, another outlaw who rode with Quantrill during the Civil War. In 1868 she gave birth to her first child, Rosie Lee (better known as Pearl). In 1870 Reed was on the run for killing the man who murdered his brother.

On November 19, 1873, Jim Reed and Belle Starr robbed a Creek Indian, Watt Greyson, of $30,000 in gold, and paper currency. Belle said, "Mrs. Greyson began to cry as soon as she saw us, screaming loudly for help. I approached her bed, placed my revolver on her forehead and said: 'One word more and I will blow your brains out.'"

When Watt refused to tell them the location of his treasure, Belle found a rope, tied his legs, and fashioned a noose. "We hoisted him to the branch of an oak; he began to strangle, and signed to us to take him down. Thereupon he showed us his hiding place."

Returning to Texas, Belle held up a stage with her husband, James Reed. They made off with $3,000 of the stage line's money and another $2150 they collected from the passengers. They were discovered later that day having supper at an Inn and had to fight their way out.

Jim Reed rode off with a friend, John Morris, in August of 1874. They stopped at a farmhouse for supper, and Morris somehow convinced Reed to leave his guns outside with the horses. Morris made an excuse to go outside while they were eating, grabbed his Winchester from his saddle, and shot Reed dead at the supper table.

The story is Morris did it to collect the reward money on Jim Reed's head. Because nobody in the area knew Reed, the officials dragged Belle out to the farm house to identify her husband. Belle didn't want Morris to get the reward, so when the sheriff lifted the sheet covering her husband's body, she shook her head and said it wasn't him. "John Morris shot the wrong man."

They buried Jim Reed in a pauper's field, and no reward money was ever paid out.

In 1877 Blue Duck, an outlaw said to be Belle's common law husband, borrowed $2,000, and dropped it all on the gambling tables in Fort Dodge,

Kansas. When he told Belle, she was furious and said she wasn't having any of that. Belle strapped on her pistols and headed for Fort Dodge. She crept upstairs at the "gambling hell," and took $7,000 at gunpoint from a private poker game.

When Belle found herself running low on money again, he prettied herself up and acted like a lady. She attended church and Sunday school, and within a short time, she was wooed by a middle-aged bank cashier. Belle visited him one day when he was alone at the bank. When she was sure no one else was around, Belle whipped out her revolver, and a bag— and demanded he fill it with cash, or else.

After he had handed her the money, Belle warned the cashier to keep quiet until she made her getaway, or she'd fill him full of lead. Belle jumped on a horse she had waiting at a nearby livery stable and rode off into Indian Territory.

Belle married Sam Starr, a Cherokee half-breed, in 1880, and set up house in a remote area of Indian Territory. They had a run-in with the law for stealing horses, and in 1882, Belle and Sam got sentenced to a year in the Detroit House of Corrections, by Hanging Judge, Isaac C. Parker.

Belle got arrested again for horse theft in midsummer of 1886. She was taken to Fort Smith and acquitted in September of the same year. An article published in *The Dallas Morning News* on June 7, 1886, described Belle as she was awaiting trial. "Belle attracts considerable attention where she goes, being a dashing horse-woman, and exceedingly graceful in the saddle. She dresses plainly…is of medium size, well formed, a dark brunette, with bright and intelligent black eyes."

That same article said, "When at home, her companions are her daughter, Pearl…her horse, and her two trusty revolvers, which she calls her *babies*."

In 1886 Sam Starr was caught in the crossfire while being chased and shot in the head. Fortunately, it was only a scratch. He managed to grab a rifle and shoot his way out. On Belle's advice, Sam turned himself in. At the trial, Sam started an argument with a member of the posse. The next thing you know, it erupted into a gunfight. Sam got shot and killed.

Two years later, on February 3rd, 1889, Belle was killed in ambush riding home from a neighbor's house. She took four buckshot in the back, three in the head, and one in the neck. The blast knocked her off her horse. When she was down the attacker came in for the kill, and blasted her in the face and neck with turkey shot.

Edgar Watson was the main suspect. He had recently had an argument over some farm property he rented from Belle. He was arrested, tried, and released. Not long after that, he received fifteen years in prison for horse theft.

BIBLIOGRAPHY

Alexander, General E. P. "Pickett's Charge and Artillery Fighting at Gettysburg." *The Century Magazine* January 1887: 464 - 471.

Alexander, H. H. *The Life of Guiteau and the Official History of ... the Trial of the Guiteau For Assassinating Pres. Garfield.* 1882.

Ambrose, Stephen E. *Crazy Horse, and Custer: The Parallel Lives of Two American Warriors.* 2012.

Anderson, Rasmus B. *The Norse Discovery of America.* 1906.

Armstrong, Perry A. *The Sauks and the Black Hawk War with Biographical Sketches, etc.* 1887.

Balderston, George Canby, and Lloyd. *The Evolution of the American Flag.* 1909.

Blue, Corinne J. Naden and Rose. *Belle Starr and the Wild West.* 2000.

Brackenridge, Hugh Henry. *Incidents of the Insurrection in the Western Parts of Pennsylvania, in the Year 1794.* n.d.

Buchanan, James. *Mr. Buchanan's Administration on the Eve of the Rebellion.* 1866.

Buel, J. W. *Heroes of the Plains, or Lives and Wonderful Adventures of Wild Bill, Buffalo Bill, Kit Carson, Capt. Payne, "White Beaver," Capt. Jack, Texas Jack, California Joe and Other Celebrated Indian Fighters, Scouts, Hunters and Guides.* 1891.

—. *Life and Marvelous Adventures of Wild Bill the Scout.* 1880.

—. *The Border Outlaws.* 1884.

Calhoun, John C. *The South Carolina Exposition.* 1832.

Carrington, Henry B. *Battles of the American Revolution, 1775 - 1781: Historical and Military Criticism with Topographical Illustration.* 1876.

Casas, Bartolomé de las. *A Brief Account of the Destruction of the Indies.* 1561.

Crawford, Captain Jack. "The Truth About Calamity Jane." *The Journalist* 5 March 1904.

Dacus, J. A. *Illustrated Lives and Adventures of Frank and Jesse James and the Younger Brothers - The Noted Outlaws.* 1881.

Donald, Jay. *Outlaws of the Border: A Complete and Authentic History of the Lives of Frank and Jesse James and Their Robber Companions, Including Quantrell and His Noted Guerillas.* 1883.

Estleman, Loren D. *Aces, and Eights: The Legend of Wild Bill Hickok.* 2010.

Etulain, Richard W. *The Life, and Legends of Calamity Jane.* 2014.

Frothingham, Richard. *Battle of Bunker Hill.* 1890.

Garland, Hamlin. "Custer's Last Fight As Seen By Two Moon." *McClure's Magazine* September 1898: 443 - 448.

Garrett, Pat. *The Authentic Life of Billy the Kid.* 1882.

Haley, W. D. "Johnny Appleseed - A Pioneer Hero." *Harper's New Monthly Magazine* November 1871: 830-837.

Harman, S. W. *Hell On the Border.* 1898.

Hayey, Henry Gillespie. *A Complete History of the Life and Trial of Charles Julius Guiteau, Assassin of President Garfield.* 1882.

Hensel, W. U. *Buchanan's Administration on the Eve of the Rebellion.* 1908.

Hewes, George R. T. *Traits of the Tea Party.* 1835.

Hoeper, George. *Black Bart: Boulevardier Bandit.* 1995.

Hogeland, William. *The Whiskey Rebellion: George Washington, Alexander Hamilton, and Frontier Rebels Who Challenged America's Newfound Sovereignty.* 2010.

Holland, Henry W. *William Dawes and His Ride with Paul Revere.* 1878.

Hudd, Alfred E. *Richard Ameryk, and the Name America.* 1910.

Hudd, Alfred E. "Richard Ameryk and the name America." *Proceedings of the Clifton Antiquarian Club* 1909 - 1910: 8 - 24.

Hunt, General Henry J. "The Battle of the First Day at Gettysburg." *The Century Magazine* November 1886: 112 - 133.

—. "The Second Day at Gettysburg." *The Century Magazine* December 1886: 278 - 296.

—. "The Third Day at Gettysburg." *The Century Magazine* January 1887: 451 -464.

Jane, Calamity. *The Life and Adventures of Calamity Jane.* 1896.

John Mitchinson, John Lloyd. *The Book of General Ignorance.* 2006.

Jucovy, Linda. *Searching for Calamity Jane: The Life and Times of Calamity Jane.* 2012.

Jung, Patrick J. *The Black Hawk War of 1832.* 2008.

Kearns, Doris. *Team of Rivals: The Political Genius of Abraham Lincoln.* 2006.

Law, General E. M. "Round Top and the Confederate Right at Gettysburg." *The Century Magazine* December 1886: 296 - 306.

Levene, William Collins, and Bruce. *Black Bart: The True Story of the West's Most Famous Stage Coach Robber.* 1992.

Lossing, Benson J. *The Pictorial Field-Book of the Revolution (2 Volumes).* 1860.

Maynard, Nettie Colburn. *Was Abraham Lincoln a Spiritualist?* 1891.

McLaird, James D. *Calamity Jane: The Woman and the Legend.* 2005.

—. "Calamity Jane: The Life and Legend." *South Dakota History* 1994.

Moore, Frederick. "How Buffalo Bill Won His Name." *The Wide World Magazine* May 1903: 42 - 47.

Morgan, Robert. *Lions of the West: Heroes and Villans of the Westward Expansion.* 2012.

Nichols, George Ward. "Wild Bill." *Harper's New Monthly Magazine* February 1867.

O'Donoghue, Denis. *The Voyage of St Brendan the Abbot.* 1893.

Patterson, W. G. "Calamity Jane A Heroine of the Wild West." *The Wide World Magazine* September 1903: 450 - 457.

Prentiss Ingraham, M. D. Ruggles, and Edward P. Doherty. "Pursuit and Death of John Wilkes Booth." *The Century Magazine* 1890 January: 443 - 449.

Ridge, John Rollin. "The Life and Adventures of Joaquin Murrieta." 1854.

Rosa, Joseph G. *Wild Bill Hickok: The Man and His Myth.* 1996.

Saint-Germain, C. de. *The Dalton Brothers and Their Astounding Career of Crime.* 1892.

Scott, Richard. *Eyewitness to the Old West: Firsthand Account of Exploration, Adventure, and Peril.* 2002.

Severin, Timothy. *The Brendan Voyage.* 2010.

Shirley, Glenn. *Belle Star: The Literature, The Facts, and The Legend.* 2014.

Siringo, Charles. *History of Billy the Kid.* 1920.

Slaughter, Thomas P. *The Whiskey Rebellion: Frontier Epilogue to the American Revolution.* 1988.

Smith, John. *Generall Historie of Virginia.* 1632.

Spurr, Howard W. *The Paul Revere Album.* 1903.

Stevens, Frank Everett. *The Black Hawk War.* 1903.

Swaney, Burton T. Hoyle and Homer H. *Lives of James A. Garfield and Chester A. Arthur with a Brief History of the Assassin.* 1881.

Swett, S. *History of the Bunker Hill Battle with a Plan.* 1826.

Thatcher, John Boyd. *Christopher Columbus: His Life, His Work, His Remains.* 1904.

Thwaites, Reuben Gold. *The Story of the Black Hawk War.* 1892.

Townsend, George Aldred. *The Life Crime and Capture of John Wilkes Booth.* 1865.

Townsend, George Alfred. "How Wilkes Booth Crossed the Potomac." *The Century Magazine* April 1884: 822 -832.

Tripp, C. A. *The Intimate World of Abraham Lincoln.* 2006.

Varigny, C. De. *The Women of the United States.* 1895.

Vespucci, Amerigo. *Mundus Novus Letter to Lorenzo Pietro Di Medici.* 1916.

Wakefield, John Allen. *History of the Black Hawk War.* 1856.

Weik, Jesse W. "A New Story of Lincoln's Assassination." *The Century Magazine* February 1913: 559 - 562.

AUTHOR'S NOTE

everal websites were instrumental in researching and writing this book.

Google Books and Project Guttenberg give researchers and writers access to first editions of many works it would take endless hours to track down. Several of the links in the eBook versions of this book link to those sources.

Another great reference tool is Chronicling America: Historic American Newspapers. It offers full page reproductions of thousands of American newspapers first published between 1836 and 1922. You can search by state, subject, and date range, so it makes it easy to find the information you need.

I didn't link to the newspapers I quoted in this book, but all quotes are attributed to individual papers so you can track down the original article if you would like to read more.

If you're looking for old magazine articles, one of the best sources is Making of America from the Cornell University Library. The site offers thousands of digitized journal articles from 1831 – 1901. Highlights of the collection include full runs of *Harper's New Monthly Magazine*, *The Century Magazine*, and *Scribner's Magazine*. The site also offers a digitized collection of Civil War Documents that includes the Official

Records of the Union and Confederate Navies and the Official Record of the War of the Rebellion.

ABOUT THE AUTHOR

Nick Vulich writes short easy to read solutions to your e-commerce problems, but now and then he likes to return to his roots: historical writing.

This book is a collection of short *historical bytes*. Some of them debunk popular myths, some talk about little known historical events, or approach well-known events from a different perspective.

Everything in this book is true. No names have been changed to protect the innocent—or guilty. Any conversation included within quotes is authentic and taken from contemporary sources. I've tried my hardest to stick to the facts. Many times, it is impossible to distinguish truth from fiction because there are so many competing accounts. In those cases, I've tried to stick with the version "the experts" say is true. Believe me, I understand—there are at least two sides to every story. Some readers are going to disagree with my choices, and that's the way it should be. History is fluid, and we reinterpret the facts from generation to generation.

Just remember, there are two sides to every story, and what you choose to believe depends on your perspective.

BONUS EXCERPT

(If you like western history, you're going to love my newest book—Dead Men and Dollar Bills, When the Daltons Rode in Kansas. *It's a fast-paced history of the Dalton Gang, their rise, and eventual fall. This chapter sizes up the gang members.)*

To the casual observer, the boys appeared to be a group of ranch hands or a posse of deputy marshals as they rode across the prairie. There was nothing to indicate they were the most wanted band of outlaws in the Territory.

The men wore long brown overcoats and slouch hats that hung down low over their foreheads.

On their person, they carried two Colt .45 revolvers—one on the hip, and another in a shoulder holster. Bob carried another revolver in his boot. But the gang's weapon of preference was the most recent model Winchester. It was an outlaw's best friend at close or long range.

There were never more than ten members of the gang. They included Emmett, Bob, and Grat Dalton, Bill Doolin, George "Bitter Creek" Newcomb, "Blackface" Charley Bryant, Charley Pierce, Bill Power (also spelled as Powers in many accounts), Dick Broadwell, and William McElhanie.[1]

Grat was the original badass. He could be a bit pugnacious and enjoyed nothing better than a good fight. He was oldest (of the outlaw boys), so his soul remained undiluted. His two greatest pleasures in life were drinking whiskey and playing cards. He was 27 when he cashed in his chips at Coffeyville.

Bob was as cool as a cucumber. He was quick witted and had a bit of the silver tongued devil inside of him. Similar to his brother Bill, Bob "could talk himself into and out of anything." He stood just over six-foot-tall, was a crack shot with a pistol or revolver, and, as to Bob's skill as a shootist, Charles O. Wilhite said, "he could kill a prairie chicken on the wing with a Colt's revolver."[2] In *Hell on the Border*, S. W. Harman wrote Bob Dalton "was known as a crack shot and knew no fear." He added, Emmett "rivaled his brother, Bob, in the ready use of his gun and his coolness while under fire."[3]

If you asked anyone, Bob was the guy who was going to make it. He was cool, level-headed, and fearless under fire. Unfortunately, he met his maker, at the tender, young age of twenty-two.

Emmett was the baby of the bunch when they pulled the Coffeyville job. He had just turned twenty. A reporter who interviewed Emmett after the raid said, "He is a young man with an attractive face; no man or woman would believe him a criminal did they know nothing of his career."[4] Charles O. Wilhite was doing some newspaper work in the 1890's when

---

[1] Dalton, Emmett. When the Daltons Rode. (page 103)
[2] The Evening World. October 29, 1892.
[3] Harman, S. W. Hell on the Border.
[4] Star and Kansan. October 28, 1892.

he met Bob and Emmett. He described Emmett as "rather below the medium height, but square built and wiry as a cat, had muscles of iron and phenomenal powers of endurance. But his eye, like Bob's, was forever restless."[5]

Marshall Evett Dumas Nix admired his grit. He wrote, "Emmett Dalton was fearless, and he loved excitement, but he lacked the bloodthirsty bravado of the successful bandit."[6] That would explain the way he followed Bob around like a lost puppy. Had Bob not gone astray, Emmett would likely have made a name for himself as a lawman. Instead, he crossed over to the dark side.

Bill Doolin was a good-natured cowboy, with a thatch of red hair on the top of his head, blazing blue eyes, and a big droopy mustache. Among the boys, he was known as the cowboy comedian, always cracking jokes in that slow southern drawl of his. Emmett likened Doolin to a "sinister clown" in who's big hand "a six-shooter looked like a toy."[7]

George "Bitter Creek" Newcomb (also known as the Slaughter Kid) was the runt of the litter. He was a puny little guy, weighing in at something like 135 pounds. Like Bill Doolin, he was a bit of a cut up. He laughed and joked around a lot and was never serious, but give him a Winchester or a Colt and he could do some damage. His alias—Bitter Creek—came from the lines of a song he was constantly singing. After the Adair train robbery, Bob dropped him from the gang because he was "too wild."

"Blackface" Charley Bryant got his nickname from a splotch of gunpowder burns on his face. He often talked about how he wanted to go

---

[5] The Evening World. October 29, 1892.
[6] Nix, Evett Dumas. Oklahombres, Particularly the Wilder Ones. (page 36)
[7] Dalton, Emmett. When the Daltons Rode. (page 39)

out in a blaze of glory. He had a "ravishing illness,"[8] and gang members assumed he talked that way because he'd rather go out shooting than rot away in a hospital bed. By all accounts, he was one card short of a full deck, which made him somewhat of a loose cannon and more careless than normal. He was, however, a good man with a gun and someone the boys could rely on in a pinch.

Charley Pierce was a late comer to the gang. The Adair hold up was his first, and last, job with the gang.[9] He was 27 years old at that time— the black sheep of his family. He drifted from Missouri to Oklahoma in the 1880's, and worked as a cowboy and professional horse racer. Author Harold Preece suggested he was a bit of a lady's man, and said the Daltons soon got tired of him sniffing around their women. After the Dalton Gang was wiped out in the Coffeyville raid, he became a charter member of the Doolin-Dalton Gang.

William McElhanie is somewhat of a mystery. Supposedly, he rode with the gang to New Mexico and California. On the way back, he headed out for his sister's house in Arkansas and never came back.[10] If he participated in any of the robberies, it would have been the Alila job in California. The only other thing Emmett has to say about him is he was also known as the "Narrow Gage Kid."

The fly in the ointment was Bill Dalton. He may, or may not have been a member of the original Dalton Gang. He may, or may not have been involved in the Alila and Ceres robberies. Some historians, and commentators of the day, suggested he was the banker and brains of the

---

[8] Dalton, Emmett. When the Daltons Rode. (page 91)
[9] Dalton, Emmett. When the Daltons Rode. (page 171)
[10] Dalton, Emmett. When the Daltons Rode. (page 83)

group, preferring to stay out of danger. Whether that's true or not, we will probably never know.

Whatever the case, William, or Bill, as he was most commonly known—was an enigma. The *Fort Worth Gazette* described him as "a smooth faced, pleasant looking man of stout build."[11] At the time of the boys first train job in Alila, Bill was supposed to be a respectable rancher who had aspirations of joining the California legislature.[12] If that was so, a little time with his brothers changed the course of his life.

Not long after the boys robbed their first train, Bill got himself arrested three times. He was accused of taking part in the Alila and Ceres train robberies. One newspaper article speculated, "Bill Dalton is supposed by everyone in the Southwest to have been the banker for his brothers, willing to share the benefits of their raids, but unwilling to brave the dangers." They went on to say, "William likes to parade his pistols where he thinks there is no danger."[13] The implication of course, was he was a bit of a rabble rouser, and a coward.

After the boys were wiped out in the Coffeyville raid, Bill's mouth pretty near got him strung up. Just days after the shoot-up, he told reporters "the boys were wrong in trying to rob the banks, but were right when they shot the men trying to kill them."[14] Next, he instituted a lawsuit against

---

[11] Fort Worth Gazette. October 7, 1892.
[12] Galveston Daily News. October 7, 1892. Most sources say Bill Dalton was at one time a member of the California legislature, but there are no records to back this up. This article says "he is an ex-member of the California legislature and was a man of prominence until his brothers robbed a Southern Pacific train in Tulare County and he was arrested as an accomplice..." This article could have started that rumor.
[13] Pittsburg Dispatch. December 26, 1892.
[14] Abilene Weekly Reflector. October 27, 1892.

the city, claiming they stole $900 from his brother Bob's dead body.[15] Not satisfied with that, he opened a lawsuit against Deputy Marshal Ed Chapman, saying he stole the horse Emmett rode into Coffeyville on. Bill was lucky he wasn't back shot, or strung up, considering the tense mood in Coffeyville in the days following the robbery.

All the while Emmett lay at death's door the girls of Coffeyville brought bouquets of flowers to decorate his room. In a matter of days, the attitude of the townspeople went from hate to a sort of morbid respect for young Emmett. Bill Dalton, on the other hand, came under closer scrutiny. One newspaper wrote, "Will's actions and words and his bank account are all interesting straws to watch when considering the question of his silent partnership in the firm of 'Dalton brothers, bandits and outlaws.' Whose business cards should have borne the inscriptions: 'Train and bank robbing a specialty.'"[16]

Soon—very soon—there would be no doubt which side of the law Bill Dalton stood on.

Bill did a total 360, hooked up with Bill Doolin and formed the Doolin-Dalton Gang, better known as the Wild Bunch. If you thought the original Dalton Gang was tough, these guys made them look like a bunch of school girls.

---

[15] Wichita Daily Eagle. November 3, 1892. The article says Bill Dalton claims $9000 was removed from Bob Dalton's body, and he is suing for $10,000. According to Emmett Dalton, Bob actually had $900 on his person when they rode into Coffeyville.

[16] Abilene Weekly Reflector. October 27, 1892.

Made in the USA
Lexington, KY
22 March 2017